THUS I LIVED WITH WORDS

. . . .

Muse Books

The Iowa Series in
Creativity and Writing

ROBERT D. RICHARDSON

Series Editor

Thus I Lived with Words

ROBERT LOUIS STEVENSON

AND THE WRITER'S CRAFT

Annette R. Federico

UNIVERSITY OF IOWA PRESS, IOWA CITY

University of Iowa Press, Iowa City 52242

www.uipress.uiowa.edu

Printed in the United States of America

Design by Richard Hendel

The University of Iowa Press is a member of Green Press Initiative and is committed to preserving natural resources.

Printed on acid-free paper

Library of Congress Cataloging-in-Publication Data
Names: Federico, Annette, R. 1960– author.
Title: Thus I lived with words : Robert Louis Stevenson and the writer's craft / Annette R. Federico.
Other titles: Robert Louis Stevenson and the writer's craft
Description: Iowa City : University of Iowa Press, 2017. | Series: Muse books | Includes bibliographical references and index.
Identifiers: LCCN 2017005966 | ISBN 9781609385187 (pbk) | ISBN 9781609385194 (ebk)
Subjects: LCSH: Stevenson, Robert Louis, 1850–1894—Criticism and interpretation. | Authorship. | Style, Literary. | Values in literature. | Stevenson, Robert Louis, 1850–1894. | Authors, Scottish—19th Century—Biography. | BISAC: LANGUAGE ARTS & DISCIPLINES / Composition & Creative Writing. | BIOGRAPHY & AUTOBIOGRAPHY / Literary.
Classification: LCC PR5496 .F43 2017 | DDC 828.809 [B]—dc23
LC record available at https://lccn.loc.gov/2017005966

JOSEPH N. FEDERICO

1921–2017

While all the little brown birds
sing upon the spray

—RLS

Dear reader, I deceive you with husks,
the real works and all the pleasure are
still mine and incommunicable.
—Robert Louis Stevenson to
  W. E. Henley, March 13, 1884

CONTENTS

PREFACE

. . . .

Robert Louis Stevenson (1850–1894) was one of the most popular and prolific writers of the late nineteenth century, an era of mass readership and literary celebrity. Stevenson was and was not a part of that world. He didn't seek publicity, but he never turned away interviewers, fellow artists, or autograph-seekers. He wasn't a close confederate of London's literary elite, and he wrote for the market; yet he held himself to the highest professional standards. Probably the least petty, least competitive author of his generation, Stevenson was unusually open to literary collaboration, even when he suspected it could damage his reputation. Always supportive of young writers, he delighted in offering advice and encouragement; but he was honest about the sacrifices required for success. Stevenson was celebrated as a brilliantly epigrammatic writer and a master stylist, yet he was perfectly willing to revise or condense his work. He routinely read drafts aloud to his family to get their feedback, which he always respected (he even burned the first draft of *Jekyll and Hyde* when his wife objected to it). An American publisher recorded, with some surprise, that Stevenson "was not handicapped by the superstition that his copy was divine revelation and that his words were sacrosanct."[1]

In his letters, Stevenson could carry on about his ideas and plans for books with both enthusiasm and candid self-doubt. He celebrated when he got paid, but he refused payment when he felt his work was not his best. Stevenson was also a perceptive literary critic whose capacity for reading was almost superhuman. He admired, and he judged. But he never belittled.

Stevenson tried his hand in virtually every genre: short stories, novels, poetry, essays, travel writing, and drama. He had a vagabonding nature and seemed game for anything, despite chronic ill health. Though he was a well-educated gentleman, he wore collarless shirts and loose jackets because he thought he'd be more likely to pursue an adventure if he weren't worried about his clothes. For adventure was Stevenson's idiom. "I have been after an adventure all my life," he wrote in 1879, "a pure dispassionate adventure, such as befell early and heroic voyagers."[2] His writing and his life were braided together by this theme of hopeful voyaging, of eventfulness.

. . . . . .

In an essay on the elements of style in literature, Stevenson cautioned that he was about to embark on the "distasteful business" of demystifying the artist's craft. "There is nothing more disenchanting to man than to be shown the springs and mechanism of any art. All our arts and occupations lie wholly on the surface; it is on the surface that we perceive their beauty, fitness, and significance; and to pry below is to be appalled by their emptiness and shocked by the coarseness of the strings and pulleys." He thought that to talk about the mechanics of writing was like "taking down the picture from the wall and looking on the back," or "pulling the musical cart to pieces" like a curious child.[3]

Yet as a consummate technician and professional man of letters, Stevenson liked nothing better than gossiping about how writers handled literary problems. He was, in fact, always prying below the surface, looking on the back of the picture, indulging a meddling curiosity about literary nuts and bolts. He had taught himself to write by studying the methods of great writers, and he felt that he had much to teach others. But he also understood that no art could be explained diagnostically to any aspirant, whether professional or amateur. If it could be, it wouldn't be art. There are both "conscious and unconscious artifices," he wrote—rhythms and harmonies that "lie too deep in nature and too far back in the mysterious history of man."[4] In this book, I have tried to balance the springs and mechanisms with the emotional and the mysterious parts of literary writing, as RLS practiced it.

THUS I LIVED WITH WORDS

....

R L S

I n the 1960s, old gas lamps from the streets of Edinburgh, Scotland, were removed and sold, mainly to scrap collectors and antique dealers from the United States, in preparation for the city's conversion to electric street lighting. More than 85,000 lamps were taken down, although a few in the closes—the narrow lanes and backstreets in Edinburgh's medieval Old Town—were refitted with sodium lighting. An article on the transition in the *Glasgow Herald* reported that the old lamps, cleaned and burnished, were valuable commodities, creatively refashioned into novelty lights or "indoor plant containers."[1] There was some discussion about whether historically noteworthy streetlamps would be preserved. One lamp in particular was singled out: the one at the door of 17 Heriot Row, Robert Louis Stevenson's childhood home in Edinburgh's New Town, an elegant south-facing street across from Queen's Street Gardens. It is the gas lamp he made famous in "The Lamplighter," from *A Child's Garden of Verses*:

> My tea is nearly ready and the sun has left the sky;
> It's time to take the window to see Leerie going by;
> For every night at teatime and before you take your seat,
> With lantern and with ladder he comes posting up the
>   street.
>
> Now Tom would be a driver and Maria go to sea,
> And my papa's a banker and as rich as he can be;
> But I, when I am stronger and can choose what I'm
>   to do,

O Leerie, I'll go round at night and light the lamps with
   you!

For we are very lucky, with a lamp before the door,
And Leerie stops to light it as he lights so many more;
And O! before you hurry by with ladder and with light,
O Leerie, see a little child and nod to him to-night![2]

This portrait of a child's fancy is quietly grounded in the
actual. In the 1870s, unlike today, the lamps on Heriot Row
were spaced far apart. The Stevensons *were* very lucky to
have one before their door. And because Edinburgh's lamplighters were tightly supervised during their beat, Leerie
really did have to "hurry by with ladder and with light" to ful-
fill his nightly quota. Stevenson recalled how "the lamplighters took to their heels every evening, and ran with a good
heart. It was pretty to see man thus emulating the punctu-
ality of heaven's orbs; and though perfection was not absolutely reached, and now and then an individual may have
been knocked on the head by the ladder of the flying func-
tionary, yet people commended his zeal in a proverb, and
taught their children to say, 'God bless the lamplighter!'"
It's quite believable that a child, even one from a well-off
family, might wish to follow in Leerie's romantic profession.
The glowing gas lamps were like "domesticated stars," the
lamplighter a mythical being "distributing starlight." Here
was a little Prometheus "knocking another luminous hole
into the dusk."[3]

. . . . . .

The "quavering and flaring" of the wilderness of Edinburgh's
street lamps in gusty weather, the way they "begin to glitter along the street" at dusk, the "humming, lamplit city,"
"the lamps springing into light in the blue winter's even"[4] —
the sight must have penetrated Stevenson's consciousness,
for it appears in his writing fairly often, a piece in the mo-

saic of Scotland, childhood, and home to complement the incessant rain, his nurse Alison Cunningham's fire-and-brimstone stories (he called her Cummy), and the summers spent at his grandfather's manse in Colinton, just outside Edinburgh, where boys hid bull's-eye lanterns under their coats, part of some lost childhood game. Louis, as he was called, seemed from an early age to have had both a powerful bent toward the marvelous and a love of the concrete, printed word. "Men are born with various manias; from my earliest childhood, it was mine to make a plaything of imaginary series of events; and as soon as I was able to write, I became a good friend to the paper-makers."[5]

As a boy he was afflicted with a series of ailments: scarlet fever, bronchitis, gastritis. He had horrid nightmares he could recall well into adulthood. It's unsettling to remember that some of the most charming children's poems ever written were composed in a darkened room at his house, La Solitude, in Hyères, France, after an attack of opthalmia left Stevenson, in his early thirties, temporarily blind; he wrote lefthanded on paper pinned to a board, his right arm bound to his body because of lung hemorrhaging. The world of *A Child's Garden of Verses* is ordinary, middle-class life made wonderful by a child's wonder—nightmares tamed by music. But Stevenson's instinct for the charming had a harrowing undertow. Lamplight casts long shadows. Leerie's ladder had its random victims.

Stevenson was called to the things of this world, as all writers have to be if they're interested in telling stories about it. He had a mind that could transform raw sensory data and scraps of memory into meaningful and unforgettable images. The poems in *A Child's Garden of Verses* are lyrical versions of Stevenson's essays on dogs, umbrellas, beggars, talking, walking, waiting, reading, writing, and the weather. He was an avid and reverent observer of materiality, and it is the clarity and vividness of his writing that make his stories so extraordinary. Mention Robert Louis Stevenson to some-one over fifty, and it's as though you've turned on a switch in their memory.

G. K. Chesterton noted that Stevenson had "in the devouring universalism of his soul, a positive love for inanimate objects such as has not been known since St. Francis called the sun brother and the well sister. We feel that he was actually in love with the wooden crutch that Silver sent hurtling in the sunlight" in *Treasure Island*.[6] In an age of realism, RLS pitched romance and the fiction of adventure. He had a distaste for novels that harped on "life's dulness and man's meanness," and felt that to "draw a life without delights" is proof of professional incompetence.[7] "Vital; that's what I aim at first: wholly vital, with a buoyancy of life," he wrote in one letter. "Then lyrical, if it may be, and picturesque, always with an epic value of scenes, so that the figures remain in the mind's eye forever."[8]

As a young man, before he became "R.L.S.," Louis played the part of a literary gypsy, complete with long hair and velvet jacket. When they first met at the Savile Club, in London, Henry James described Stevenson as a "pleasant fellow, but a shirt-collarless Bohemian and a great deal (in an inoffensive way) of a *poseur*."[9] It was not entirely a pose. His closest friend and literary executor, Sidney Colvin, recalled that originally Louis wore his hair long "from the fear of catching cold. His shabby clothes came partly from lack of cash, partly from lack of care, partly ... from a hankering after social experiment and adventure, and a dislike of being identified with any special class or caste."[10] Louis was dead serious about being a writer. He gently satirized the real poseurs, the clubmen and the aesthetes, "those young eaglets of glory, the swordsmen of the pen, who are the pride and wonder of the world.... They are all clever authors; and some of them, with that last refinement of talent, old as Job but rare as modesty, have hitherto refrained from writing." These young clubmen, always "rising" to fame, never

......

4

actually get down to *work*, never write anything anyone can understand and enjoy.[11]

Stevenson never forgot his readers. He didn't want to develop, in the fashionable phrase of the day, an "artistic temperament," which, after all, does not "make us different from our fellow-men, or it would make us incapable of writing novels."[12] What he wanted was to become a writer, maybe even a great writer. He didn't pretend to be a genius, though he knew he had certain gifts. He came to think of himself as a toiler and a craftsman, and he was happy in those roles. His advice to writers was split equally between practical, tool-sharpening strategies and moral encouragement. He told others, as he told himself, not to think for a moment of fame or success. "Write as much as you can, and as slowly and carefully as you can," he advised one young author. "And keep up a good heart."[13] "Do not think of distinction, but find pleasure in your work from day to day," he urged another.[14] For Stevenson, it was one long apprenticeship. When he was in his early thirties, he wrote to Will H. Low, "Eight years ago, if I could have slung ink as I can now, I should have thought myself well on the road after Shakespeare; and now—I find I have only got a pair of walking shoes and not yet begun to travel."[15]

Stevenson set out to learn the literary trade as a kind of wager with himself, the way someone might take up juggling or "learn to whittle."

All through my boyhood and youth I was known and pointed out for the pattern of an idler; and yet I was always busy on my own private end, which was to learn to write. I kept always two books in my pocket, one to read, one to write in. As I walked, my mind was busy fitting what I saw with appropriate words; when I sat by the roadside, I would either read, or a pencil and a penny version-book would be in my hand, to note down the features of the scene or commemorate some halting stanzas. Thus I lived with words. And what I thus wrote was for no ulterior use, it was written consciously for practice. It was not so much that I wished to be an author (though I wished that too) as that I had vowed that I would learn to write.[16]

Stevenson gave himself exercises in description, he created dialogues, he kept diaries. Most significantly, as he remembered, he studiously impersonated authors he admired, ventriloquizing their stylistic habits and memorable turns of phrase. "I have thus played the sedulous ape to Hazlitt, to Lamb, to Wordsworth, to Sir Thomas Browne, to Defoe, to Hawthorne, to Montaigne, to Baudelaire and to Obermann."[17] At the age of thirteen, he worked on satiric portraits of the residents of Peebles, Scotland, after Thackeray's *Book of Snobs*. He tried his hand at an epic in the style of Keats and moral essays after John Ruskin. He wrote a stage drama in imitation of Alexandre Dumas (an author he never stopped admiring). Of course, he failed again and again—he was barely out of his teens, after all. Yet through these exercises, Stevenson said, "I got some practice in rhythm, in harmony, in construction and the co-ordination of parts."[18] He developed a feel for good writing and for what makes an author's style interesting and pleasurable to the reader. "Think of technique when you rise and when you go to bed," he advised one young artist. "You have not to represent the world. You have to represent only what you can represent with pleasure and effect, and the way to find out what that is [is] by technical exercise."[19] Reading and rereading the best authors, living with the sound and sense of their prose, and aping them sedulously was the springboard for Stevenson's literary education. "That, like it or not, is the way to learn to write."[20]

Stevenson came from a family of famous lighthouse engineers—lamplighters on a larger scale. When he was seventeen, Louis spent four months on the Scottish coast studying the trade, or at least the poetic side of it. In "The Education of an Engineer," he described his frame of mind at the time:

> I came as a young man to glean engineering experience from the building of the breakwater. What I gleaned, I am sure I do not know; but indeed I had already my own private determination to be an author; I loved the art of words and the appearances of life; and *travellers*, and *headers*, and *rubble*, and *polished ashlar*, and *pierres perdues*, and even the thrilling question of the *string-course*, interested me only (if they interested me at all) as properties for some possible romance or as words to add to my vocabulary.

He soaked it all in, "the sunshine, the thrilling seaside air, the wash of waves on the sea-face, the green glimmer of the divers' helmets far below, and the musical chinking of the masons." Indeed, he was eager to try diving, and twenty years later described the experience in splendid prose and with astonishing physical detail. But his "one genuine pre-occupation" at the time was when he was not on duty. Then he drew in his chair and "proceeded to pour forth literature, at such a speed, and with such intimations of early death and immortality, as I now look back upon with wonder."[21]

One simple exercise he practiced was description, for "to any one with senses there is always something worth describing, and town and country are but one continuous subject."[22] But what an impossible assignment! He wrote to his cousin Bob in these years that nature is "far too complex for our comprehension, how much more for our description: five square feet of Scotch hillside would take a man a lifetime to describe, and even then how lame, how empty: after he had chronicled heather, whin, bracken, juniper, grass, these little yellow flowers and the rest, it would only be to find that each of these objects taken separately are [*sic*] indescribable, and that their combination is as much above human powers as flying."[23] Five years later he wrote to Mrs. Frances Sitwell from France, "I tried for long to hit upon some language that might catch ever so faintly the indefinable shifting colour of olive leaves; and above all, the changes and little silverings that pass over them, like blushes over a face, when the wind tosses great branches to and fro."[24] Stevenson's early letters are bursting with descriptive vignettes, as though he had to capture in language every impression that possessed him—"the sight of people and things has pursued me," he will write, or "[t]hese are some of the things that took hold of me."[25] "I am never satisfied, you understand, but long and long and long to do something with the beauty that I see, and I don't know what to do."[26] Such are the dreams of an ambitious young man. Yet Louis obviously grasped very early how essential it was for a writer to hold onto sensory details, to pay attention. There are, of course and alas, gifts that come only from the gods: "Passion, wisdom, creative force, the power of mystery or colour, are allotted in the hour of birth, and can be neither learned nor simulated."[27] But other essential talents may be acquired, with a little effort.

RLS liked to make fun of his propensity to sermonize on almost any subject, a trait he acquired from his maternal grandfather, who was a Presbyterian minister. So he had plenty of advice for anyone who asked about the art of writing: read widely, study other authors, aim for simplicity, have a consistent focus, work on a style, cut out the twaddle, keep a stout heart. He could be both encouraging and brutal. To his cousin Katharine de Mattos, who had sent him a sample of her work, he wrote, "I am going to be rude. It's all bad. It is woolly, hard to follow, and disorderly. You should not have begun with a question; never put yourself so far into the reader's power: you don't come to him for instruction." He advised her not to be in a hurry. "Now, all this you *cannot* do just now; you have to learn to write first a good deal better. Do you understand me, when I say you are writing with gloves on just now; you must learn to write with the quick of your fingers."[28] "Writing is a habit like fencing; but a little harder, because there are more passes possible, and more parries and returns," he wrote to another student, Charles Robertson. "It is fencing with a hundred rapiers at once." He thought that too many beginners fail to trust their own experiences. They begin with a hypothesis, when they should begin with a fact. "The point is this. It's not *enough about anything*. It's all in the air—like a kite," he complained to Robertson. Readers are interested in what's down here, on the ground, what's recognizable to them. The beginner, he said, "refrains as with a fevered caution from communicating his experience," yet in the last resort, "experience, whether about life or a man's own mind, is the only thing worth hearing, indeed is the only thing anyone can have to tell upon his own authority." For young author Robertson, he had three bits of advice:

First. *Look about you in India and see what you see.* Now, mark you, what *you* see, not what others have shown you. Think about your own experiences in the same way. Second. Try your pen on a little sharp detail; tackle a scene or a face that strikes you, and try what you can make of it in pen and ink. Third. Give up for the moment theoretical writing. You can come back to that after you have learned (first) to see with your own eyes and (second) to write with your own docile pen.[29]

For a while Stevenson gave free writing lessons to a young woman determined to become an author. He pulled no punches. "I never in my life read a worse description," he told her during one of their sessions.

You should have used fewer adjectives and many more descriptive verbs. If you want me to see your garden, don't, for pity's sake, talk about 'climbing roses' or 'green mossy lawns.' Tell me, if you like that roses twined themselves round the apple trees and fell in showers from the branches. Never dare to tell me anything ever again about 'green grass.' Tell me how the lawn was flecked with shadows. I know perfectly well that grass is green. So does everybody else in England. What you have to learn is something different from that. Make me see what it was that made your garden distinct from a thousand others. And, by the way, while we are about it, remember once and for all that *green* is word I flatly forbid you to utter in a description more than, perhaps, once in a lifetime.

Having lived through that phase of criticism from a master of English letters, Miss Adelaide Boodle could carry on her efforts with courage and resolution. "For after all, R.L.S. *'was going* to teach me to write.' What on earth did anything else matter?"[30]

. . . . . .

Stevenson made himself write something every day. "I believe in the covering of much paper: each time with a definite and not too difficult artistic purpose," he wrote. "Thus one progresses."[31] His own progress in the profession of letters was slow but determined. He began his career placing essays in magazines, publishing by the end of his life about a hundred literary essays. He was a truly great short story writer. But most of his projects were never finished or never started. By one count, there are only twenty-seven principle works of the 393 items projected in a compendium of Stevenson's letters and notebooks, although some were gathered into collections later or published posthumously. He wrote that "the succession of defeats lasted unbroken till [he] was thirty-one," when he published *Treasure Island* in a boys' magazine.[32] Until the success of *Strange Case of Dr. Jekyll and Mr. Hyde*, in 1886, and before the royalties started to come in from *Treasure Island* and *Kidnapped*, Stevenson was constantly short of money. He always had

. . . . . .

several jobs going on at once. He haggled with publishers, fought for copyrights, struggled to meet deadlines. When he had to, he used his friends and connections to get a foot in the door. "Nobody had ever such pains to learn a trade as I had," he wrote in 1887, "but I slogged at it, day in, day out; and I frankly believe (thanks to my dire industry) I have done more with smaller gifts than almost any man of letters in the world."[33]

One thing Stevenson had done was point English literature in another direction from the one in which it was heading. His romance and adventure tales swam against the tide of late-nineteenth-century realism and the school of Emile Zola, fiction imported from France that was naturalistic and documentary in its treatment of social problems and human misery. RLS did not care for M. Zola, although he was a lifelong Francophile. He admired Hugo, Balzac, Villon, and Jules Barbey d'Aurevilly; he was a worshipper of Dumas, a devout pupil of Montaigne, and a strong advocate of his friend, Auguste Rodin, whose severe and amoral sculptures confused British art critics. He shook hands with Flaubert and Zola as fellow artists of uncontested genius. But their meticulous scrutiny of the seamier side of human experience was very far from his conception of the purpose of literature. Art should *reverse* our usual way of seeing the world, not duplicate it. "The business of real art," Stevenson wrote, is "to give life to abstractions and significance and charm to facts."[34] To please, to charm, to add decoration to life, "to satisfy the nameless longings of the reader, to obey the ideal laws of the day-dream"[35]—this was the writer's true calling.

RLS usually wrote in a bed propped up with pillows, an image that became iconic when Stevenson modeled for the American sculptor Augustus Saint-Gaudens in 1887 (it was even embossed on the covers of later editions of his works). The books that made him famous—*New Arabian Nights, Treasure Island, A Child's Garden of Verses, Strange Case of Dr. Jekyll and Mr. Hyde, Kidnapped, The Master of Bal-*

lantrae—were written in Scotland, England, the south of France, Saranac Lake, and the Pacific islands. Chronically ill for most of his life, suffering frequent episodes of pulmonary hemorrhages, blood-spitting, nausea, fevers, and nervous disorders, Stevenson was always looking for a suitable climate. His friends expressed astonishment at his stoicism. Henry James marveled that volumes that draw "so strong a current of life ... have largely been written in bed, in dreary 'health resorts,' in the intervals of sharp attacks. There is almost nothing in them to lead us to guess this."[36] For Stevenson, it was just life, and as he often claimed, life was a heroic wrangle with failure. He insisted that it isn't happiness we are pursuing but meaningfulness, a feeling of aliveness to experience itself. "Nor is happiness, whether eternal or temporal, the reward that mankind seeks," he wrote to Edmund Gosse. "Happinesses are but his wayside campings; his soul is in the journey; he was born for the struggle and only tastes his life in effort and on the condition that he is opposed."[37] To John Addington Symonds, he wrote, "Men do not want, and I do not think they would accept, happiness; what they live for is rivalry, effort, success."[38] The year before he died, he wrote to the great English novelist George Meredith, "For fourteen years I have not had a day's real health; I have wakened sick and gone to bed weary; and I have done my work unflinchingly. I have written in bed, and written out of it, written in hemorrhages, written in sickness, written torn by coughing, written when my head swam for weakness; and for so long, it seems to me I have won my wager and recovered my glove.... I was made for a contest, and the Powers have so willed that my battlefield should be this dingy, inglorious one of the bed and the physic bottle. At least I have not failed, but I could have preferred a place of trumpetings and the open air over my head."[39]

To the dismay of his parents and friends, when Louis was twenty-nine he took off for America in pursuit of Mrs. Fanny Van de Grift Osbourne, a woman he had met at an

......

artist colony near Grez-sur-Loing, France, two years earlier. Fanny was an American divorcée with two children, and she was ten years older than Stevenson. But she was clearly The One. He embarked on a ship from Greenock to New York, then took an emigrant train across the United States to San Francisco to meet her. He later wrote about the experience in *The Amateur Emigrant*. Louis and Fanny honeymooned at an abandoned mining cabin in Calistoga, California, the subject of *The Silverado Squatters*, then traveled across the Atlantic, spending time in France and Scotland. Finally settling at a house in Bournemouth, England, Stevenson named it Skerryvore after the tallest lighthouse in Scotland, built by his uncle Alan Stevenson. It was where he wrote *Dr. Jekyll and Mr. Hyde*, inspired by a dream. The family crossed the Atlantic once again for Louis's health, to stay at a highly respected sanatorium in Saranac Lake, New York. He didn't know it, but it was the last time he would see the Old World and the last he would see of Edinburgh—"the venerable city which I must always think of as my home."[40] "I will say it fairly, it grows on me with every year," he wrote from America, "there are no stars so lovely as Edinburgh street-lamps."[41]

. . . . . .

Stevenson loved being at sea. "Fine, clean emotions; a world all and always beautiful; air better than wine; interest un-flagging: there is upon the whole no better life."[42] During the subfreezing winter when he was at Saranac Lake, Stevenson signed a lucrative contract with Scribner's to write a series of letters about a six-month yachting cruise of the Pacific islands. He departed from San Francisco with his extended family in 1888, eventually traveling to the Marquesas, the Paumotus, Tahiti, Honolulu, Auckland, the Tokelau Islands, Cook Islands, Ellice Islands, Gilbert Islands, Marshall Islands, and New Caledonia. By the end of 1890, Stevenson and his entourage had settled in Apia, Samoa. "The sea,

. . . . . .

islands, the islanders, the island life and climate, make and keep me truly happier," he wrote to Henry James.[43] He and Fanny built a house, Vailima Estate, on four acres of weedy tropical forest. The Samoans gave RLS the name Tusitala, "The Teller of Tales."

Despite considerable pleasure and interest in this new scene, Stevenson's letters in the last four years of his life often convey sadness and exhaustion. Fanny's mental health was volatile. He had difficult relationships with some of the white settlers on Apia. Mail from Europe was at times aggravatingly slow. With forty now behind him, Stevenson felt old. How had writing become suddenly so difficult, so galling? He marveled at his rate of production when he was younger: "And to think I took this up because I thought it was easy!"[44] He had fatal writer's block, false starts, crises of confidence that the trash he was laboring over would sink his reputation. As always, he worried about money to support his family and to pay for Vailima. So he kept churning it out.

Stevenson died on December 3, 1894, less than a month after his forty-fourth birthday. He was in a good mood. He had been working hard on another Scottish novel, *Weir of Hermiston*, and felt buoyantly confident about it. He told his stepdaughter, Belle, who had been acting as his amanuensis, "It will be my best work; I feel myself so sure in every word!"[45] He and Fanny were making mayonnaise for a dinner salad, when suddenly he said, "Do I look strange?" Then he collapsed. He died three hours later of a brain hemorrhage.

It was, incredibly, the way Stevenson wanted to die—standing up in his clothes, as he said to Fanny, in the middle of doing something, not growing old and helpless and lying in a sickbed. "I wish to die in my boots; no more land of counterpane for me."[46] He was buried on the top of Mount Vaea, as he had requested. Forty Samoan laborers cut a road to the top, some of them from Stevenson's own household in

Vailima. "His life had been one long romance," wrote Fanny, "and he hoped to have a romantic end; the artist in him demanded that completeness."[47]

In Samoa, the "tame celebrity," as he called himself, received mail from autograph seekers, fledgling authors, writers offering inscribed editions, and, of course, fellow Scots. He got involved in Samoan politics and was critical of European imperialist ambitions in the South Seas. The stories he began to send to his London publishers in this period anticipate the works of Joseph Conrad in their moral vision. Some of his correspondents in Britain didn't understand this change in Stevenson. They grew impatient with his preoccupation with "native politics, prisons, *kava* feasts," as Colvin put it, "and such things as our Cockney stomachs can ill assimilate."[48] They wanted back the old RLS, the yarns, the pirates, the Highland adventures. He had been thinking for a long time about doing a sequel to *Kidnapped*, this time with a heroine at the center. Friends expressed delight when he finally published *Catriona* in 1893. "Oh, he's a miracle of a lad, that boy out there in the Cannibal Islands," wrote the painter Edward Burne-Jones. "I wish he would come back and write only about the Borderland."[49]

RLS always meant to return to Scotland and to Edinburgh. He wrote in *The Silverado Squatters* about how inscrutable his feeling for home seemed. "There is no special loveliness in that gray country, with its rainy, sea-beat archipelago; its fields of dark mountains; its unsightly places, black with coal; its treeless, sour, unfriendly looking cornlands; its quaint, grey, castled city, where the bells clash of a Sunday, and the wind squalls, and the salt showers fly and beat."[50] Yet there was a part of his heart that still drew him there. Brooding on Scotland and his childhood brought up "a whole decameron of little stories."[51] "I am one of the few people in the world," he wrote to Henry James, "who do not forget their own lives."[52] When he settled in Apia, Stevenson began a series of long journal letters to Sidney Colvin.

He kept them going until the year he died. In one, dated June 1893, he wrote about the rain—a running theme in Stevenson to match his streetlamps. The rain crops up in the evening prayers he wrote for the household at Vailima, in *A Child's Garden of Verses*, in his Scottish fiction. He once remarked to Henry James, "Nobody has done justice to rain in literature yet: surely a subject for a Scot."[53] In the letter to Colvin, Stevenson wrote, "It pours with rain from the westward, very unusual kind of weather; I was standing out on the little verandah in front of my room this morning, and there went through me or over me a heave of extraordinary and apparently baseless emotion. I literally staggered. And then the explanation came, and I knew I had found a frame of mind and body that belonged to Scotland, and particularly to the neighbourhood of Callander."[54] Callander is a town near Stirling, at the gateway to the Highlands, where the Stevensons took a house for part of the summer when he was about sixteen. His mother wrote in her diary at that time, "Lou has his pony and enjoys himself."[55]

The rain raining all around, on the umbrellas in Edinburgh, on the ships at sea, in the Samoan tropics—it was one experience. A writer has to believe that his life and emotions contain a comprehensive relevance to other lives, that there may be something universal about at least some human feelings and desires. The German philosopher Walter Benjamin, in 1936, mourned the loss of the storyteller after the devastation of World War I. Modernity, he thought, was dominated by information and testable facts because modern people were unable to speak about their own experiences anymore; they had become inscrutable to themselves. "More and more often there is embarrassment all around when the wish to hear a story is expressed. It is as if something that seemed inalienable to us, the securest among our possessions, was taken from us: the ability to exchange experiences." The storyteller reaches back through his own lifetime and the lifetimes of others, through hearsay, legend, word of mouth, and his own boundless imagination. "His gift is the ability to relate his life; his distinction, to be able to tell his entire life. The storyteller: he is the man who could let the wick of his life be consumed completely by the gentle flame of his story. This is the basis of the incomparable aura about the storyteller."[56]

During a decade in which a disheartened world was occupied by very serious matters, it seems remarkable that Benjamin would single out Robert Louis Stevenson as one representative of this invaluable and gifted tribe. Stevenson deeply responded to the pull of stories, just as he understood the need for continuity through generations, which Benjamin believed was so important in a fragmented world. In his dedication at the beginning of *Catriona*, published the year before he died, Stevenson wrote, "And I have come so far, and the sights and thoughts of my youth pursue me, and I see like a vision the youth of my father, and of his father, and the whole stream of lives flowing down there far in the north, with the sound of laughter and tears, to cast me out in the end, as by a sudden freshet, on these ultimate islands. And I admire and bow my head before the romance of destiny."[57]

A feeling for the past and the reach of his own history must have haunted Stevenson in 1893, for a similar thought, a bit less formally expressed, came out in the letter to Colvin that I began with. "Very odd these identities of sensation, and the world of connotations implied," Stevenson wrote. "Highland huts and peat smoke, and the brown swirling rivers, and wet clothes, and whisky, and the romance of the past, and that indescribable bite of the whole thing at a man's heart, which is—or rather lies at the bottom of—a story."[58]

ROMANCE

L ike a lot of people, when he felt restless or sulky or especially when he was too sick or run down to work, Stevenson looked for something to read that would both relax and stimulate him. "When I suffer in mind, stories are my refuge; I take them like opium; and I consider one who writes them as a sort of doctor of the mind." Serious art—Shakespeare, George Eliot, even Balzac—won't do the trick. In these moods he needs

> old Dumas, or the *Arabian Nights*, or the best of
> Walter Scott; it is stories we want, not the high
> poetic function which represents the world.... We
> want incident, interest, action: to the devil with your
> philosophy. When we are well again, and have an easy
> mind, we shall peruse your important work; but what
> we want now is a drug. So I, when I am ready to go
> beside myself, stick my head into a story-book, as the
> ostrich with her bush.[1]

He liked to complain that there was nothing good to read in his cynical and prosaic age; contemporary fiction was either deadly serious or intolerably clever. "The great lack of art just now is a spice of life and interest; and I prefer galvanism to acquiescence in the grave." Novels about modern life were "like mahogany and horse-hair furniture, solid, true, serious, and as dead as Caesar."[2] After a severe illness in 1884 when he was stuck in bed for days, Stevenson was desperate for a fix: "But I do desire a book of adventure—a romance—and no man will get or write me one," he complained to W. E. Henley. "I want to hear swords clash. I want a book to begin in a good way.... O my sighings after romance, or even Skeltery, and O! the weary age which will produce me neither!"[3]

Skeltery was Stevenson's coinage for the old-fashioned, melodramatic staginess of his bygone and beloved *Skelt's Juvenile Drama*, a toy theater made of paper cutouts, plain and colored, that he purchased from a stationer's shop in the Leith Walk, Edinburgh. He played with Skelt addictively. Skelt "stamped himself upon my immaturity" and planted in his soul "the very spirit of my life's enjoyment."[4] Skelt magnetized his young imagination and colored his world with glamour. If you accept G. K. Chesterton's theory, *Skelt's Juvenile Drama*, with its pasteboard figures, castles, inns, and bright, contrasting colors, even had a part in the development of Stevenson's style, such as his attraction to stark, vivid images and his "love of sharp edges and cutting or piercing action." "It was because he loved to see on those lines, and to think in those terms," observed Chesterton, "that all his instinctive images are clear and not cloudy; that he liked a gay patch-work of colour combined with a zigzag energy of action, as quick as the crooked lightning. He loved things to stand out; we might say he loved them to stick out; as does the hilt of a sabre or the feather in a cap."[5] Chesterton asserted that if there is one real sentence of autobiography in Stevenson's works, it is from his essay on *Skelt's Juvenile Drama*, "'A Penny Plain and Twopence Coloured'": "What am I? what are life, art, letters, the world, but what my Skelt has made them?"[6] Maybe this is a disarming bit of hyperbole, thrown out for effect in a lighthearted memoir; and it's unwise to speculate too much about the psychological sources of any artist's work. Yet Stevenson also privately confessed his great delight in revisiting his favorite childhood pastime. "Give me an early proof of Skelt," he begged his editor. "I love, I love that paper."[7]

. . . . . .

Skeltery is of "those direct clap-trap appeals, which a man is
dead and buriable when he fails to answer; of the foot-light
glamour, the ready-made, bare-faced transpontine picturesque."[8] It is an old wayside inn where "gentlemen in three-
cocked hats" play at bowls, or "dank gardens that cry aloud
for a murder," or certain rocky coasts set apart for shipwreck,
and the words "post-chaise," "the great North Road," "ostler,"
"nag"—words, Stevenson said, that "still sound in my ears
like poetry."[9] Any story that is rich in incident and largely
pictorial, that is morally interesting, deals with human passions, and is driven by imaginative energy has a bit of Skeltery to it. These are the tales that have been touched by *romance*, that talismanic word for Stevenson, incorporating
style and method, pleasure and moral purpose, everything
in literature and in life he cared about most—password into
the hidden nucleus of most people's lives.

Serious-minded people, in Stevenson's age and our own,
have a tendency to denigrate stories of romance and adventure as escapist. They think an engrossed reader is in a
dangerous trance. But a person may be more concentrated
and aroused when he is reading a novel than when he is
going about his daily business. Something has restored his
imagination and startled him awake. In his essay on Walt
Whitman, Stevenson wrote that the artist should resuscitate
people from the "stupefying ... recurrence of unimportant
things." Once in awhile, we should "rise to take an outlook
beyond daily concerns, and comprehend the narrow limits
and great possibilities of our existence."[10] Everyone should
be mentally kidnapped once in a while and spirited away
from everyday routine—from newspapers and ubiquitous
electronic devices, especially. And one of the best portals to
elsewhere has been and always will be a gripping good yarn.

To certain tastes—to Stevenson's, certainly—what is desired is the clatter of hoofs along a moonlit lane, an armful

of pistols and a ship under siege, or the flight of fugitives through the Scottish heather.

So there we stood, side by side upon a small rock slippery with spray, a far broader leap in front of us, and the river dinning upon all sides. When I saw where I was, there came on me a deadly sickness of fear, and I put my hand over my eyes. Alan took me and shook me; I saw he was speaking, but the roaring of the falls and the trouble of my mind prevented me from hearing; only I saw his face was red with anger, and that he stamped upon the rock. The same look showed me the water raging by, and the mist hanging in the air: and with that I covered my eyes again and shuddered.

The next minute Alan had set the brandy bottle to my lips, and forced me to drink about a gill, which sent the blood into my head again. Then, putting his hands to his mouth, and his mouth to my ear, he shouted, "Hang or drown!" and turning his back upon me, leaped over the farther branch of the stream, and landed safe.

I was now alone upon the rock, which gave me the more room; the brandy was singing in my ears; I had this good example fresh before me, and just wit enough to see that if I did not leap at once, I should never leap at all. I bent low on my knees and flung myself forth, with that kind of anger of despair that has sometimes stood me instead of courage. Sure enough, it was but my hands that reached the full length; these slipped, caught again, slipped again; and I was sliddering back into the lynn, when Alan seized me, first by the hair, then by the collar, and with a great strain dragged me into safety.

Never a word he said, but set off running again for his life, and I must stagger to my feet and run after him. I had been weary before, but now I was sick and bruised, and partly drunken with the brandy; I kept stumbling as I ran, I had a stitch that came near to overmaster me;

and when at last Alan paused under a great rock that stood there among a number of others, it was none too soon for David Balfour.[11]

I fell under the spell of *Kidnapped* when I was in my twenties, and I've reread it many times since. It is a little jewel. Dame Hilary Mantel (winner of two Man Booker Prizes, author of *Wolf Hall* and eleven other novels) has said that *Kidnapped* is perfection. "There's nothing in it that shouldn't be there, nor is it lacking anything. I know Stevenson modestly said it was just a story for boys, but it's actually a perfect novel."[12] Stevenson found the period of the story—Scotland in the 1750s, following the Jacobite Rebellion—marvelously picturesque. He knew the setting of the novel well from his trips to the Hebrides and Highlands, and he advised readers to get out a map and walk in David's footsteps if they didn't trust his geography—which some people, including Dame Hilary, still do today. Many of the characters were based on real people, and the crime at the center of the story, the Appin murder, is an historical fact. Yet Stevenson wrote in his dedication to *Kidnapped*, "It is more honest to confess at once how little I am touched by the desire of accuracy." Instead he was after "a book for the winter evening schoolroom when the tasks are over and the hour for bed draws near," something "to steal some young gentleman's attention from his Ovid, carry him awhile into the Highlands and the last century, and pack him to bed with some engaging images to mingle with his dreams."[13] He wanted to appeal to the reader's sense of wonder, not to the scholar's interest in facts. The "crown and triumph of the artist," he wrote, is "not to be true merely, but to be lovable; not simply to convince, but to enchant."[14]

Theodore Watts-Dunton, in an 1886 review of *Kidnapped*, noted that in every work of fiction, the author passes through two stages. The first is when the situation is "invented," which usually has to do with the plot; and the second is when the tale is "really imagined, when the inventor's mind has become as familiar with them as though he had actually lived in them. Not till it has reached the latter stage can imaginative work in any art become vital and, so to speak, organic."[15] *Kidnapped* is packed with these kinds of imagined, lived-in scenes. Stevenson was casual at first about this novel. He said it began "partly as a lark, partly as a pot-boiler," a bit of Highland adventure to fetch the boys and make a few pounds. But then "suddenly it moved, David and Alan stepped out from the canvas, and I found I was in another world."[16]

Stevenson was very good at creating memorable characters, yet he found it one of the trickiest parts of writing fiction. In the essay "Some Gentlemen in Fiction," he wrote, "[T]o make a character at all—so to select, so to describe a few acts, a few speeches, perhaps (though this is quite superfluous) a few details of physical appearance, as that these shall all cohere and strike in the reader's mind a common note of personality—there is no more delicate enterprise, success is nowhere less comprehensible than here." If a writer were to record verbatim the racy speech of any man he'd just met, he'd be surprised at how dull and insignificant it would come off. "Physical presence, the speaking eye, the inimitable commentary of the voice, it was in these the spell resided; and these are all excluded from the pages of a novel." He went on in the essay to present an author of his acquaintance—clearly RLS himself—who remarked on the curious palpability of his characters:

> "In one of my books," he writes, "and in one only, the characters took the bit in their mouth; all at once, they became detached from the flat paper, they turned their backs on me and walked off bodily; and from that time, my task was stenographic—it was they who spoke, it was they who wrote the remainder of the story. When this miracle of genesis occurred, I was thrilled with

joyous surprise; I felt a certain awe—shall we call it superstitious? And yet how small a miracle it was; with what a partial life were my characters endowed; and when all was said, how little did I know of them! It was a form of words that they supplied me with; it was in a form of words that they consisted; beyond and behind was nothing."[17]

These thin-air people, constructed of nothing but language—how is it they seemed to live in time and occupy space?

When he couldn't wait for such a miracle of composition, Stevenson tried impersonation or ventriloquism to get his people moving. Fanny related how, once, he rushed into her room for a mirror because he wished to capture "a certain haughty, disagreeable expression" of James Durie's, in *The Master of Ballantrae*, and was disconcerted when he saw his own reflection instead of "the master's clean-shaven face and powdered head."[18] When he dictated his novels, Belle reported that he sometimes played the different parts of the characters, impersonating their accents and gestures, even pronouncing some words in broad Scots.[19] He almost *enacted* his stories as he imagined them.

Many readers wondered at *Kidnapped*'s picturability, its vividness to the eye, its palpability. Edmund Gosse thought it "one of most human books I ever read. The only romance I know in which the persons have stomach-aches and sore throats."[20] Henry James praised the central portions of *Kidnapped* for their "singular pictorial virtue: these passages read like a series of inspired footnotes on some historic page."[21] Yet as a novelist, Stevenson seemed less interested in conjuring pictures than in creating kinetic movement. In an illuminating letter to Stevenson about *Catriona*, James wrote, "The one thing I miss in the book is the note of *visibility*—it subjects my visual sense, my *seeing* imagination, to an almost painful underfeeding. The *hearing* imagina-

......

tion, as it were, is nourished like an alderman, ... so that I seem to myself ... in the presence of voices in the darkness — voices the more distinct and vivid, the more brave and sonorous, as voices always are — but also the more tormenting and confounding — by reason of these bandaged eyes."[22] RLS replied, "Your jubilation over *Catriona* did me good, and still more the subtlety and truth of your remark on the starving of the visual sense in that book. 'Tis true, and unless I make the greater effort — and am, as a step to that, convinced of its necessity — it will be more true I fear in the future." Stevenson's way into a tale was different from that of James, who was better at presenting nuances of behavior and feeling, a character's psychological complexity. James was especially sensitive in representing women's inner lives, a class of character Stevenson was almost afraid to touch; and fully realized women are glaringly absent in Stevenson's oeuvre. Stevenson's gift was for a cinematic sense of speech, movement, and focalization: the chapter with David and Alan on the rock is strikingly cinematic, for example, even down to its auditory details. "I *hear* people talking and I *feel* them acting," he wrote to James,

> and that seems to me to be fiction. My two aims may be described as —
>   *1st* War to the adjective.
>   *2nd* Death to the optic nerve.
>   Admitted we live in an age of the optic nerve in literature. For how many centuries did literature get along without a sign of it?

He concluded, politely — after all this *was* Henry James — "However I'll consider your letter."[23]

Stevenson believed, as an article of faith, that a writer should always address both the reader's imaginative cravings and his moral interest. The greatest works of literature satisfy a natural and enduring appetite for the dramatic.

Fashions come and go, he wrote to Henley, but "under any fashion, the great man produces beauty, terror and mirth, and the little man produces cleverness (personality, psychology etc.[*sic*]) instead of beauty, ugliness instead of terror, and jokes instead of mirth."[24] An exotic locale is not requisite for romance. The "truth to the conditions of man's nature and the conditions of man's life, the truth of literary art ... may be told us in a carpet comedy, in a novel of adventure, or a fairy tale. The scene may be pitched in London, on the sea-coast of Bohemia, or away on the mountains of Beulah." What matters most is work that is "conceived with honesty and executed with communicative ardour."[25] "To deal with strong and deadly elements, banditti, pirates, war and murder, is to conjure with great names," but a fresh and stirring impression may be created from smaller events.[26] Stevenson even tipped his hat to Jane Austen: "Elizabeth Bennet has but to speak, and I am at her knees."[27]

Stevenson didn't like a one-sided treatment of human experience, and he didn't think readers needed to be immolated under unsavory truths. The possibility of beauty should not be sacrificed to a writer's dexterity or to a "scientific thoroughness" committed to communicating "matter which is not worth learning."[28] A writer who thinks truth is found only in the sordid side of things—a boring conversation or a stinking mews—is incomplete as an artist, even as a realist. "[H]arping on life's dulness and man's meanness is a loud profession of incompetence," he insisted. "To draw a life without delights is to prove I have not realised it."[29]

Yet Stevenson knew that a writer who thinks truth is only discoverable in wildly extravagant plots or indulgent fantasies may very likely turn out work that is inert. Romance does not mean falsifying the facts of life or running away from them. Stevenson was certainly a realistic person, if not a writer of realistic fiction. He grew up between the Shorter Catechism of Scotch Presbyterianism and the bombardments of Darwinian science. He looked death in the face on more than one occasion and was profoundly aware that human suffering must be faced without the consolations of religion or the belief in an afterlife—what he once called a "fairy tale of an eternal tea-party."[30] But he felt that despite the discouraging appearance of things, most people desire what's right and accept the idea of duty as a guidepost. They go on "obscurely fighting the lost fight of virtue." They have, simply, a "desire of good."[31] The greatest romances do not offer consolation for unhappiness or escape from the perplexities of real life. Just the reverse is true. In a romance, the reader's judgments and feelings about life are intimately and intensely engaged. Romance pitches the reader out of himself into something greater, and so touches something nearly universal. "The fortune of a tale lies not alone in the skill of him that writes, but as much, perhaps, in the inherited experience of him who reads; and when I hear with a particular thrill of things that I have never done or seen, it is one of that innumerable army of my ancestors rejoicing in past deeds."[32] Stevenson grasped the importance of kindling ancient memories borne by generations of readers who have warmed their hands against myth and legend, as far back as time itself. Especially in a society dominated by science and statistics, he demanded stories with "incident that woos us out of our reserve."[33] "Thus novels begin to touch not the fine *dilettanti* but the gross mass of mankind, when they leave off to speak of parlours and shades of manner and stillborn niceties of motive, and begin to deal with fighting, sailoring, adventure, death or child-birth; and thus ancient outdoor crafts and occupations, whether Mr. Hardy wields the shepherd's crook or Count Tolstoi swings the scythe, lift romance into a near neighbourhood with epic."[34] For the danger for the contemporary author in the age of realism, said Stevenson, "is lest, in seeking to draw the normal, a man should draw the null, and write the novel of society instead of the romance of man."[35]

In "The Lantern-Bearers," one of his best-known essays, Stevenson linked his thoughts about fiction with his observations about the inscrutability of people's inner lives—rich, colorful lives, if one could see the romance that animates them. The story of the boys with the bull's-eye lanterns hidden under their coats is a moving metaphor for how we experience the self and how we should imagine others. "Justice is not done to the versatility and the unplumbed childishness of man's imagination. His life from without may seem but a rude mound of mud; there will be some golden chamber at the heart of it, in which he dwells delighted."[36] This secret place of delight is what the writer must address. If he misses this, he misses everything. The psychologist William James, who had a special affection for Stevenson's writing, thought "The Lantern-Bearers" deserved immortality. To his younger brother Henry, he wrote that it was "one of the most beautiful things ever written."[37] Stevenson understood and respected the emotional and psychological needs of his readers because they were his own needs. He anticipated by half a century the work of intellectuals such as Carl Jung, D. W. Winnicott, and John Dewey, who saw that creative activity and a free imagination are critical to self-growth. "Fiction is to the grown man what play is to the child," said Stevenson. "It is there that he changes the atmosphere and tenor of his life."[38]

In an essay on Stevenson's art, Henry James, with typical elegance and perception, put his finger on the motive behind Stevenson's love of romance. "He would say we ought to make believe that the extraordinary is the best part of life even if it were not, and to do so because the finest feelings— suspense, daring, decision, passion, curiosity, gallantry, eloquence, friendship—are involved in it, and it is of infinite importance that the tradition of these precious things should not perish."[39] The noblest literature deliberately and skillfully involves the reader's deep-seated feelings, in all their variousness. "Not only love, and the fields, and the bright face of danger," Stevenson wrote, "but sacrifice and death and unmerited suffering humbly supported, touch in us the vein of the poetic." These are the beckonings of Skeltery, adventure, romance—the open doors of the imagination. "These are notes that please the great heart of man."[40]

SIMPLICITY

....

A brother is slain in a duel in the pitch of night, the scene lit only by tall candles set upon the frozen ground. "I have left him lying beside the candles," says the servant Mackellar before he runs from the house of Durrisdeer to recover the Master's body.

From quite a far way off a sheen was visible, making points of brightness in the shrubbery; in so black a night it might have been remarked for miles; and I blamed myself bitterly for my incaution. How much more sharply when I reached the place! One of the candlesticks was overthrown, and that taper quenched. The other burned steadily by itself, and made a broad space of light upon the frosted ground. All within that circle seemed, by the force of contrast and the over-hanging blackness, brighter than by day. And there was the bloodstain in the midst; and a little farther off Mr. Henry's sword, the pommel of which was of silver; but of the body, not a trace. My heart thumped upon my ribs, the hair stirred upon my scalp, as I stood there staring—so strange was the sight, so dire the fears it wakened. I looked right and left; the ground was so hard, it told no story. I stood and listened till my ears ached, but the night was hollow about me like an empty church; not even a ripple stirred upon the shore; it seemed you might have heard a pin drop in the county.[1]

When Stevenson wanted an image of sharp contrast, he stuck with ordinary words—black, blackness, brightness, brighter, light. Not a single word in this vivid passage is long, showy, or foreign. Mackellar even describes his trepidation in familiar clichés: "my heart thumped," "empty as a church," "you might have heard a pin drop." To avoid clichés like the plague is a decree in all creative writing workshops, but Stevenson knew what he was doing. In the preface he invented to frame *The Master of Ballantrae*, the imaginary editor (initials "R.L.S.") singularly praises the "baldness" of Mackellar's narration and refuses to "work up the scenery" or "improve the style." Although he had some trouble hitting Mackellar's voice, it turned out to be a likable one to Stevenson. Indeed, the editor of the preface sounds rather Stevensonian when he claims, "I would have all literature bald."[2] When his stepdaughter Belle once asked for a definition of literature, Stevenson replied, "words used to the best purpose—no waste, going tight around a subject."[3]

Stevenson got the idea for *The Master of Ballantrae* one freezing winter night walking on the verandah of his cottage at Saranac Lake. He had just finished rereading Frederick Marryat's *The Phantom Ship* and, "moved by the spirit of emulation," wondered if he could make a similar tale "of many years and countries, of the sea and the land, savagery, and civilisation."[4] The characters in *The Master* are so uncanny, the plot so impossible, the whole thing so rapturously strange you can miss how carefully designed it is. Stevenson thought a novel must be like thread running merrily off a reel. But to craft a story demands directness, restraint, a purposeful and uncluttered method. Striking situations and dramatic dialogue, he wrote to James, "are prepared by deliberate artifice and set off by painful suppressions."[5] Perhaps more than anything else, good prose demands careful choice of detail. Realism forces detail; romance suppresses it.[6]

. . . . . .

Laboring under the shadow of Honoré de Balzac (1799–1850), influential founder of European realism, mid-

. . . . . .

Victorian authors strove to be "true to life." To this laudable end, they tended to accumulate details to the point of absurdity. One of Balzac's novels opens with this *long* description of a room:

> The paneled walls of that apartment were once painted some color, now a matter of conjecture, for the surface is incrusted with accumulated layers of grimy deposit, which cover it with fantastic outlines. A collection of dim-ribbed glass decanters, metal discs with a satin sheen on them, and piles of blue-edged earthenware plates of Touraine ware cover the sticky surfaces of the sideboards that line the room. In a corner stands a box containing a set of numbered pigeon-holes, in which the lodgers' table napkins, more or less soiled and stained with wine, are kept. Here you see that indestructible furniture never met with else-where, which finds its way into lodging-houses much as the wrecks of our civilization drift into hospitals for incurables. You expect in such places as these to find the weather-house whence a Capuchin issues on wet days; you look to find the execrable engravings which spoil your appetite, framed every one in a black varnished frame, with a gilt beading round it; you know the sort of tortoise-shell clock-case, inlaid with brass; the green stove, the Argand lamps, covered with oil and dust, have met your eyes before. The oilcloth which covers the long table is so greasy that a waggish externe will write his name on the surface, using his thumb-nail as a style. The chairs are broken-down invalids; the wretched little hempen mats slip away from under your feet without slipping away for good; and finally, the foot-warmers are miserable wrecks, hingeless, charred, broken away about the holes. It would be impossible to give an idea of the old, rotten, shaky, cranky, worm-eaten, halt, maimed, one-eyed, rickety, and ramshackle condition of the

furniture without an exhaustive description, which would delay the progress of the story to an extent that impatient people would not pardon.[7]

Balzac was a brilliant writer, no question. But he had a tendency to describe interiors, as one British reviewer put it, "with the precision of an appraiser."[8] Balzac even chides *himself* for not getting on with it! Who has patience for this kind of thing? Stevenson admired much in Balzac, but he thought his writing was "smothered under forcible-feeble detail." Because Balzac "could not consent to be dull," he became dull. "He would leave nothing undeveloped," Stevenson wrote to his cousin Bob, "and thus drowned out of sight of land amid the multitude of crying and incongruous details. Jesus, there is but one art: to omit! O if I knew how to omit, I would ask no other knowledge."[9]

Although detail should be kept under control, Stevenson did value accuracy. "My stories are not the truth, but I try to make my characters act as they would act in life. No detail is too small to study for truth," he told Belle. He and his stepson, Lloyd, "spent five days weighing money and making calculations for the treasure found in 'The Wrecker.'"[10] He read many books about North America in the 1700s when he was working on *The Master of Ballantrae*. It's *excessive* specificity that is the trapdoor, the quicksand, the quagmire for all serious writers, and what drowns "our little passionate story . . . in a deep sea of descriptive eloquence or slipshod talk."[11] "How to get over, how to escape from, the besotting *particularity* of fiction," Stevenson complained to James. "'Roland approached the house; it had green doors and window blinds; and there was a scraper on the upper step.' To hell with Roland and the scraper!"[12] It was the same with dialogue. We "turn our back upon the larger, more various, and more romantic art of yore. A photographic exactitude in dialogue is now the exclusive fashion; but even in the ablest hands it tells us no more—I think it even tells us less—than

Molière, wielding his artificial medium, has told to us and to all time of Alceste or Orgon, Dorine or Chrysale."[13] He liked one broad, theatrical stroke rather than many fine touches, terse and biting dialogue rather than meticulously observed drawing-room repartee.

Description itself was not the problem. Writing should be descriptive. Some of his favorite authors—Dumas, Hugo, Scott, Meredith—were abundantly descriptive. And Stevenson wrote some very detailed, very descriptive passages himself. But he tried to do so always with a larger end in mind, perhaps to establish a frame or strike the keynote. In his essay on Victor Hugo, for example, he explained that although the reader forgets the specific details in all those pages describing the cathedral in *The Hunchback of Notre Dame*, they were not pages thrown away. Hugo accomplished what he desired, for Notre Dame "permeates and possesses the whole book with astonishing consistency and strength," and the story is attached to that building from the first page to the last, character by character, all the way through.[14] Cumulative detail establishes the moral and emotional center of Hugo's drama, rather like Herman Melville's disquisitions on the sperm whale in *Moby-Dick*. Indeed, Stevenson called Melville "a howling cheese"—a very high compliment![15]

Nevertheless, for the serious author, overwriting is the siren's song to which he must block his ears with large gobs of wax. It is all about selection, selection, selection. "What to put in and what to leave out; whether some particular fact be organically necessary or purely ornamental; whether, if it be purely ornamental, it may not weaken or obscure the general design; and finally, whether, if we decide to use it, we should do so grossly and notably, or in some conventional disguise: are questions of plastic style continually re-arising. And the sphinx that patrols the highways of executive art has no more unanswerable riddle to propound."[16]

Stevenson knew from experience how easily a writer falls

......

in love with the flow of his own words and how difficult it is to delete material that, in itself, looks like pretty decent writing. A writer may compose an adroit dissection of a character's thoughts or strike upon an original metaphor, but if it takes away from the focus of the tale, it must be cut. He should not be enticed by extraneous matter because he's rather proud of himself. If this shortens the book, Stevenson counsels, it will probably make it better,

> for to add irrelevant matter is not to lengthen but to bury. Let him not mind if he miss a thousand qualities, so that he keeps unflaggingly in pursuit of the one he has chosen. Let him not care particularly if he miss the tone of conversation, the pungent material detail of the day's manners, the reproduction of the atmosphere and the environment. These elements are not essential: a novel may be excellent, and yet have none of them; a passion or a character is so much the better depicted as it rises clearer from material circumstance.[17]

Writers get hung up on accuracy, and so they overwrite. They forget that ruthlessly cutting out cherished bits of prose is what writing means. Stevenson was a dedicated reviser. He *liked* cutting and rewriting: "I am indefatigable at re-writing and bettering and surely that humble quality should get me on a little," he wrote to Frances Sitwell when he was twenty-three.[18] Two decades later, he thought that weeding out the pernicious liana vines from his property in Samoa seemed a good model for aspiring authors—"making a book of it by the pruning knife," clearing the book "like a piece of bush, with axe and cutlass."[19] Taming the prose is taming the ego. "You could still spend a very profitable fortnight in earnest revision and … heroic compression," Stevenson admonished Edmund Gosse. He practiced what he preached: this advice came after he detected in his own prose *three* successive sentences in blank verse! He cautioned that "one purple word is already much; three—a whole phrase—is inadmissible. Wed yourself to a clean austerity: that is your force. Wear a linen ephod, splendidly candid. Arrange its folds, but do not fasten it with any brooch. I swear to you, in your talking robes, there should be no patch of adornment."[20]

. . . . . .

The best writing achieves a pleasurable balance of sound and sense, but Stevenson would never advise adding words to make a sentence sound nice. Good prose rejects "any meaningless or very watered phrase employed to strike a balance in the sound."[21] Ornamental touches or pet phrases that have a nice ring were to RLS nothing short of heresy. A writer who's found a neat little coinage, or wants another syllable to end the sentence with a thump, is just a cheater. Miss Adelaide Boodle, Stevenson's pupil, recalled him berating another luckless disciple who was fond of *however* as "a valuable refuge from dead monotony in a poor sentence." In a broad Scotch accent, complete with rolling *r*'s, Stevenson thundered back, "'Your favourite refuge!—For-r-r-sake it, woman! For-r-r-sake it for ever! It is a r-r-refuge of lies!'"[22]

He was wary of witticisms as one especially dangerous and tempting form of clutter, probably because writers tend to think of themselves as clever types. *Wit* is different, and is concomitant with well-chosen words and balanced phrases; wit will come through without a lot of showing off, "for it is just that wit, these perpetual nice contrivances, these difficulties overcome, this double purpose attained, these two oranges kept simultaneously dancing in the air, that, consciously or not, afford the reader his delight."[23] But conscious wittiness should be avoided. He told one young author, "And the defect in manner seems to me to be a preciosity and wit in narration. Narrative style should be only witty by force of perspicuity and condensation: a touch of a quibble, or an ornament that seems not to have fallen there by accident and in pursuit of the bare fact, raises a fresh issue and steals the reader's attention from the tale. I think

. . . . . .

if you would trust more implicitly to your story, it would show its articulation better and take more hold upon the mind."[24] "In all narration there is only one way to be clever," he insisted, "and that is to be exact."[25] Rein in the quips and bons mots. Undress your prose. The masters of imaginative narrative "keep to the nude fact, and for the most part reserve their wit and flourishes for the mouths of the speakers."[26] "I like more and more naked writing," he decided.[27] Writers must "strip if we are to climb, to refuse not only facts but sentiments."[28] In short, Stevenson knew only one test of writing: "If there is anywhere a thing said in two sentences that could have been as clearly and as engagingly and as forcibly said in one, then it's amateur work."[29]

· · · · · ·

The reader of a novel doesn't want a lot of ingenious language. He wants the essential action or the striking incident. That is what "stamps the story home like an illustration." A tale stands or falls on its creation of an animated and indelible scene—"Crusoe recoiling from the footprint, Achilles shouting over against the Trojans, Ulysses bending the great bow, Christian running with his fingers in his ears, these are each culminating moments in the legend, and each has been printed on the mind's eye for ever."[30] We may forget a writer's beautiful articulations and his sparkling commentary but not the epoch-making scene. In all the essays written on his favorite authors Stevenson almost always included praise for a memorable incident or larger-than-life character; only rarely did he compliment a writer's word choice or a book's fidelity to fact. Great writing should "embody character, thought, or emotion in some act or attitude that shall be remarkably striking to the mind's eye. This is the highest and hardest thing to do in words."[31]

Compression is difficult because most writers, realists and romancers alike, have a powerful urge to capture life in words. "To hear a strain of music, to see a beautiful woman, a river, a great city, or a starry night, is to make a man despair of his Lilliputian arts in language."[32] Yet despair he must. No art can capture the actual experience of living. In this singular sense, the writer's task is hopeless, and the sooner he realizes it the better. This is why Stevenson took issue with Henry James's assertion, in "The Art of Fiction" (1884), "that the air of reality (solidity of specification) seems to me to be the supreme virtue of a novel—the merit on which all its other merits … helplessly and submissively depend." This is what produces "the illusion of life." It is here, James wrote with confidence, that the novel "competes with life."[33]

Stevenson thought James's presumptions on behalf of fiction pointed to the fundamental error of the realists, so he wrote a comeback with the mischievous title, "A Humble Remonstrance." In their desire to get all of life solidly into their novels, Stevenson insisted, the realists bury the reader alive in adjectives or drown him in the icy waters of verisimilitude. There is no "competing with life." Literature is the imposition of order against the overwhelming density of the world we live and breathe in. "Life is monstrous, infinite, illogical, abrupt, and poignant; a work of art, in comparison, is neat, finite, self-contained, rational, flowing, and emasculate." A novel is a pattern forced on the multifariousness and chaos of existence. Fiction is an exposition, a clarification. As such, it must prioritize not "solidity of specification" but a clear nerve center, an indelible aim. "And as the root of the whole matter, let him bear in mind that his novel is not a transcript of life, to be judged by its exactitude; but a simplification of some side or point of life, to stand or fall by its significant simplicity."[34]

Finally, an author can write a very long and very detailed book and still have a clean and integrated style of presentation. Stevenson admired Hugo, as we know. And how he adored Dumas! *The Three Musketeers*, *The Count of Monte Cristo*, and *The Vicomte de Bragelonne* (which Stevenson read six times, at least) are about the size of small concrete blocks. All the better for RLS. "Nay, the object of a story is to be long," Stevenson wrote to William Archer, "to fill up the hours; the story-teller's art of writing is to water out by continual invention, historical and technical; and yet not seem to water; seem on the other hand to practise that same wit of conspicuous and declaratory condensation which is the proper art of writing."[35] "For although, in great men, working upon great motives, what we observe and admire is often their complexity, yet underneath appearances the truth remains unchanged: that simplification was their method, and that simplicity is their excellence."[36]

PLAY

. . . .

I t's probably an exaggeration to say that Stevenson lived inside the literary culture of his time as a monk lives in his faith; he was too much of a free spirit for that comparison strictly to work. Yet many of his letters and essays about writing give the impression of someone in a state of rapturous bondage. Literature—reading, writing, and talking about books—was palpably Stevenson's seventh heaven.

He was always excited when he was seized by an idea for a new story. Often enough it came to nothing. But sometimes, miraculously, the scheme for a novel came happily and without a hitch. *Treasure Island* had its genesis on a rainy day in Braemar when Stevenson was playing with his stepson, Lloyd, who had taken up drawing. Stevenson created a beautifully colored map, complete with woodlands, paths, and mountains. To someone like Stevenson, a map is "a mine of suggestion." With "the unconsciousness of the predestined," he called his map "Treasure Island." "No child but must remember laying his head in the grass, staring into the infinitesimal forest and seeing it grow populous with fairy armies. Somewhat in this way," Stevenson recorded, "as I paused upon my map of 'Treasure Island,' the future characters of the book began to appear there visibly among imaginary woods; and their brown faces and bright weapons peeped out upon me from unexpected quarters, as they passed to and fro, fighting and hunting treasure, on these few square inches of a flat projection."[1] The next thing he knew he was writing out a list of chapters, and the tale took off.

His letters to W. E. Henley from September 1881, after he had cast anchor on the novel, originally titled *The Sea-Cook*, are notable for their blitheness and complacency. "It's awful fun, boy's stories; you just indulge the pleasure of your heart, that's all.... No writing, just drive along as the words come and the pen will scratch!" "I love writing boy's books. This first is only an experiment: wait till you see what I can make 'em when my hand is in." "*The Cook* is in his XIXth chapter. Yo-heave ho!" He also hoped to see some income from this venture. Stevenson was determined to "make this boy's book business pay."[2]

When an author hits his momentum, there is nothing like the joy of literary creation. At the beginning, *Treasure Island* was "quite silly and horrid fun."[3] But the tide turned. Because the story was being published serially in a boys' magazine, Stevenson had to correct page proofs for the first chapters while he was still writing the later ones. "It seems as though a full-grown, experienced man of letters might engage to turn out *Treasure Island* at so many pages a day, and keep his pipe alight," he confessed. "But alas! this was not my case." After writing a chapter a day for fifteen days, he dried up. "My mouth was empty; there was not one word more of *Treasure Island* in my bosom." Stevenson was thirty-one, he had a family, he was in poor health, and he was in debt. The proofs were coming in for the first chapters—and he had writer's block! He traveled to a retreat in Switzerland for his health, read some French novels, looked at the scenery, tried not to panic. But when he arrived at Davos, he had to return to writing. Near despair, he sat down to work on his quaint, unfinished pirate story; and by one of those mysteries of creation, the tide turned again, "and behold! it flowed from me like small talk." He was back to writing a chapter a day and, in the most "delighted industry," finished the last fourteen chapters of *Treasure Island* in two weeks.[4]

Stevenson was relieved and giddy over the completion of his first real book, by which he meant, of course, his first novel. Writing a whole novel had been an impossible, elusive dream, his "unattained ideal." He had started a dozen novels by this time in his career, with no success. "It is the length that kills," he admitted.[5] He was even more delighted that so many readers, kids and adults, were captivated by his braw yarn and his curious "puppets." Only much later did he realize that much of the first part of the story was the result of unconscious theft—that the parrot was taken from Defoe, the skeleton from Poe, and Billy Bones, the treasure chest, and "the whole inner spirit and a good deal of the material detail of my first chapters" from stories by Washington Irving. "I believe plagiarism was rarely carried farther," Stevenson admitted, yet all the time he felt the story "was original as sin; it seemed to belong to me like my right eye." No matter. With unfeigned satisfaction in what he had pulled off, Stevenson asserted that *Treasure Island* "was [his] kind of picturesque."[6]

When a writer is at the stage of outlining chapters or sketching a plot, especially if he hasn't yet had a definite success to his name, the heart beats high with courage and hope. It is a test of stamina and self-belief. "There must be something for hope to feed upon," Stevenson wrote. "The beginner must have a slant of wind, a lucky vein must be running, he must be in one of those hours when the words come and the phrases balance of themselves—*even to begin*. And having begun, what a dread looking forward is that until the book shall be accomplished! For so long a time ... you must hold at command the same quality of style; for so long a time your puppets are to be always vital, always consistent, always vigorous."[7] Stevenson usually approached creative challenges with a kind of tough exuberance—"I cannot tell you what a joy of battle, [*sic*] I have in this work."[8] But there's no question he often found writing agonizingly difficult, both mentally and physically. It got harder as he got older. The letters he wrote when he was wrestling with *The Ebb-Tide*, at age forty-three, are a far cry from those he wrote about *Treasure Island*. To read them is to suffer vicariously all the horrors of mental paralysis; Stevenson said *The Ebb-Tide* "has sown my head with grey hairs; or I believe so—if my head escaped, my heart has them."[9] When the book was finally with the publishers, Stevenson worried about reviews. *The Ebb-Tide* is a dark, uneven story about European imperialism; there's no real hero, and he felt the presentation tilted too much toward realism. But as with *Treasure Island*, he was ultimately pleased with the way the story turned out, and as always, he was glad to see some cash: "We shall hope *The Ebb-Tide* will fill the exchequer again."[10] Getting paid for his work was no small concern; as Stevenson liked to put it, "but there is Biles the butcher! Him we have always with us."[11]

. . . . . .

Stevenson was a careful, even a fastidious, writer, and he thought of himself as a craftsman. But he also viewed literature as a paid profession. Writing involved buying and selling in the marketplace, technical competency, and mastery of the trade. "For art is," he insisted, "first of all and last of all, a trade."[12] He seethed sometimes that he had "passed my days in toil, the futility of which would sometimes make my cheek to burn,—that I should spend a man's energy upon this business, and yet could not earn a livelihood."[13] He was known to complain about a public that might prefer work "a little wordy, a little slack, a little dim and knotless." Once he admitted drily to Gosse, "There must be something wrong in me, or I would not be popular."[14] But *épater le bourgeois* was not Stevenson's motto. He thought his job was to offer delight, to maintain the highest quality of writing possible, and to get paid for it. "It is doubtless tempting to exclaim against the ignorant bourgeois; yet it should not be forgotten, it is he who is to pay us, and that ... for services that he shall desire to have performed."[15]

If someone wants to be a writer, or any kind of artist, he

sooner or later has to face the question of income. "If you adopt an art to be your trade, weed your mind at the outset of all desire of money," he advised. "What you may decently expect, if you have some talent and much industry, is such an income as a clerk will earn with a tenth or perhaps a twentieth of your nervous output. Nor have you the right to look for more; in the wages of the life, not in the wages of the trade, lies your reward; the work is here the wages. It will be seen I have little sympathy with the common lamentations of the artist class."[16] Being poorly paid or well paid, going great guns or suffering agonies, setting your book afloat with flag-waving bravura or with fingers crossed that it won't be sunk by poor sales and hostile reviews — it was all in the bargain, all in a day's work. The work must be undertaken with integrity. That is understood. But Stevenson also completely comprehended that what is true in most jobs is even more true in the profession of letters: it helps not to take yourself too seriously.

· · · · · ·

A literary career is an ego-intensive profession. Writers get tied up in knots over their reputation, or they manufacture problems that are tangential to their real purpose. And so in "making or swallowing artistic formulae, or perhaps falling in love with some particular proficiency of his own, many artists forget the end of all art: to please."[17] In a letter to Edmund Gosse from 1884, while he was grappling with *Prince Otto*, Stevenson made a remarkable observation about the creative process:

> I am all at a standstill; as idle as a painted ship, but not so pretty. My romance, which has so nearly butchered me in the writing, not even finished; though so near, thank God, that a few days of tolerable strength will see the roof upon that structure. I have worked very hard at it, and so do not expect any great public favour. *In*

moments of effort, one learns to do the easy things that people like. There is the golden maxim; thus one should strain and then play, strain again and play again. The strain is for us, it educates; the play is for the reader, and pleases. Do not you feel so? We are ever threatened by two contrary faults: both deadly. To sink into what my forefathers would have called "rank conformity," and to pour forth cheap replicas upon the one hand; upon the other, and still more insidiously present, to forget that art is a diversion and a decoration, that no triumph or effort is of value, nor anything worth reaching except charm.[18]

The artist has to make his job look easy. The poet must erase from his mind the hours of study and practice he has put into perfecting his work and let it come as naturally as leaves to a tree (to steal from Keats). Stevenson was a studious formalist, but almost nothing he wrote seemed labored. Henry James expressed it perfectly when he said Stevenson "is an artist accomplished even to sophistication, whose constant theme is the unsophisticated."[19]

Strain and then play. There's something Zen about this philosophy. It describes not only a practice, but a temperament, a deliberate attitude toward one's creative work. Stevenson cultivated equipoise, a balanced disposition, something very difficult for a writer, or for anyone, to develop and maintain throughout life. In an essay about his friendship with Stevenson, Gosse wrote, "One reason it was difficult to be certain that Stevenson had reached his utmost in any direction was what I will call, for want of a better phrase, the energetic modesty of his nature. He was never satisfied with himself, yet never cast down." Gosse declared that there are "two dangers that beset the artist—the one is being pleased with what he has done, and the other being dejected with it. Stevenson, more than any other man whom I have known, steered the middle course. He never conceived that he had achieved a great success, but he never lost hope that by taking pains he might yet do so."[20] In 1884, when "intense solicitude for [his] fame" compelled his father to express distaste for one of his stories, Stevenson wrote, "Concern yourself about no failure; they do not cost lives, as in engineering.... Fame is (truly) a vapour; do not think of it; if the writer means well and tries hard, no failure will injure him, whether with God or man."[21]

If Stevenson wanted art to seem effortless, he also believed the undertaking itself should be diverting. Let's admit that writing stories is something of a frolic—as he wrote to his father, lives are not at stake here. Novelists (most of them) are not brain surgeons, or even lighthouse engineers. So however intensely he is working on his novel, the writer's efforts should be lightened by a sense of his delight in passing the hours in just that way. To borrow from the psychoanalyst D. W. Winnicott, creative work should be "deliberate but without too much of the deliberateness of trying."[22] Stevenson insisted that an author should take up his work "with the unreasoning good faith and the unflagging spirit of children at their play." He should become so involved in the pleasure of linking words together or in imagining what his characters would say and do, that it never occurs to him to ask why he is writing his story or if it is worth doing. Those questions would never "occur to the child as he plays at being a pirate on the dining-room sofa, nor to the hunter as he pursues his quarry," Stevenson wrote. "And the candour of the one and the ardour of the other should be united in the bosom of the artist."[23] The immersion of the child, the absorption of the foxhound—these are important psychological stages for creative work, and also forms of mental release, when the imagination has free rein. A writer who is not in touch with his own instinct for play and his own pleasure in playacting will ultimately fail to charm the reader. Stevenson wrote of Walter Scott, "As his books are play to the reader, so were they play to him. He conjured up the romantic with delight, but he had hardly patience to describe it. He was a great day-dreamer, a seer of fit and beautiful and humorous visions, but hardly a great artist; hardly, in the manful sense, an artist at all." Yet Scott has a lesson for the writer: "He pleased himself, and so he pleases us. Of the pleasures of his art he tasted fully; but of its toils and vigils and distresses never man knew less. A great romantic—an idle child."[24]

. . . . . .

Stevenson thought being a writer was both a wild lark and a solemn privilege. If a novelist begins his career bent on delivering wisdom, founding a new literary school, or winning awards, he will never reach into the reader's heart. RLS gave this important piece of advice to a struggling young author: "[A]nd about any art, think last of what pays, first of what pleases. It is in that spirit only that art can be made. Progress in art is made by learning to *enjoy*: that which seems a little dull at first, is found to contain elements of pleasure more largely though more quietly commingled."[25] Learning to enjoy is harder than it sounds. Sometimes even the reader has to learn to bend a little. Stevenson reported that a "servant-maid used to come and boast when she had read another chapter of *Treasure Island*; that any pleasure should attend the exercise never crossed her thoughts."[26] Neither writer nor reader should be the least bit apologetic that their shared purpose is to experience a few hours of enjoyment. Even novels that take up the most grave and earnest subjects must somehow attract and beguile.

Stevenson didn't have much patience with writers who talked about sacrificing themselves on the altar of Art. "They chose the primrose path," he wrote to Gosse. "When they found out it was not all primroses, but some of it brambly, and much of it uphill, they began to think and speak of themselves as holy martyrs. But a man is never martyred in any honest sense in the pursuit of his own pleasure."[27]

. . . . . .

He conceded that "[t]o live by a pleasure is not a high calling; it involves patronage, however veiled; it numbers the artist, however ambitious, along with dancing girls and billiard markers."[28] But neither is writing stories a calling to be ashamed of. Pleasure and play are values in and of themselves—as many wise people, from Aristotle to Wordsworth, have to keep reminding us for some reason. All that we have in us that is most excellent and most human begins in the instinct for play and for pleasure, and "the fittest lessons are the most palatable, and make themselves welcome to the mind."[29]

"No art, it may be said, was ever perfect, and not many noble, that has not been mirthfully conceived."[30] This is what authors must remember, especially when they feel like calling it quits. No one is making them write their story. They write their story because it pleases them. Far from being martyrs, writers and artists are among the luckiest people in the world. In "Letter to a Young Gentleman Who Proposes to Embrace the Career of Art," Stevenson wrote, "In the life of the artist there need be no hour without its pleasure." It's true that the writer "works in a rebellious material, and that the act of writing is cramped and trying both to the eyes and the temper." But when things are going well,

> when matter crowds upon him and words are not
> wanting—in what a continual series of small successes
> time flows by; with what a sense of power as of one
> moving mountains, he marshals his petty characters;
> with what pleasures, both of the ear and eye, he sees
> his airy structure growing on the page; and how he
> labours in a craft to which the whole material of his life
> is tributary, and which opens a door to all his tastes, his
> loves, his hatreds, and his convictions, so that what he
> writes is only what he longed to utter.

These few moments of happiness are worth all the pain and frustration. "He may have enjoyed many things in this big, tragic playground of the world; but what shall he have enjoyed more fully than a morning of successful work? Suppose it ill paid: the wonder is it should be paid at all. Other men pay, and pay dearly, for pleasures less desirable."[31]

READING

....

A letter to Miss Angela Plomer, Brisbane, Australia:

18 August [? 1893]   Vailima
Dear Madam, There are to my knowledge no "ordinary
rules"; there is certainly not one that I should be afraid
to break. I can give you in one sentence all that is
necessary. Read good authors with passionate attention;
refrain altogether from reading bad ones. Believe me,
Dear Madam, Yours truly   Robert Louis Stevenson

Miss Angela Plomer
     Brisbane

P.S. Do not think of distinction, but find pleasure in
your work from day to day.[1]

I would not blame Miss Plomer if she felt disap-
pointed in this letter or if she thought Stevenson's
counsel a little terse. But his advice, at age forty-
three, is consistent with his earliest efforts to be a
writer when he was in his teens and early twenties.
Writers rub off on one another. Read and study excellent models. Guard against shoddy writing habits that
can unconsciously creep into your work.

A significant part of any writer's career is reading other
writers, and it's doubtful anyone can "refrain altogether"
from reading bad authors. We have to read an author before it can be determined if he is bad or good—and Stevenson read his share of bad ones. At the age of thirty-seven,
he claimed that he had read thousands of novels, some of

them atrociously bad. In an interview with an Auckland reporter, he advised aspiring authors not to get mired in the work of their contemporaries except for amusement. If an author confines himself to the seventeenth and eighteenth centuries, he "will get the finest course of literature there is." He also recommended reading aloud. "Too many of us read by the eye, but the man who means to write, must, whether he articulates or not, read everything by the ear." And he thought there were two benefits to reading Latin. First it helps the writer "arrive at the value of words," and second, Latin "is capable of suggesting such extraordinary and enchanting effects, that it gives a man spur and wings to his fancy."[2]

After a while the question becomes not which books to avoid and which to read, but which to *reread*. RLS had his canon: Dumas, Meredith, Montaigne, Shakespeare, Bunyan, Scott, Hazlitt. The sedulous ape held fast to the belief that rereading and copying good writers was how to get at the marrow of their style and, perhaps equally important, how to earn a clear comprehension of their moral vision. "I never feel that I know a writer till I have tried to imitate him," he wrote to George Saintsbury.[3] A writer has to handle the tools of the trade until they feel serviceable in his own hands. Reading widely is a form of preparation, a rehearsal—like practicing the hard parts before performing the concerto, knowing the steps before getting up to dance. "Before he can tell what cadences he truly prefers, the student should have tried all that are possible; before he can choose and preserve a fitting key of words, he should long have practised the literary scales; and it is only after years of such gymnastic that he can sit down at last, legions of words swarming to his call, dozens of turns of phrase simultaneously bidding for his choice, and he himself knowing what he wants to do and (within the narrow limit of a man's ability) able to do it."[4] It takes a long time to learn how to write because *reading* takes a long time, and for Stevenson no one writes well who has not also read much. The most important word in that passage is *years*.

· · · · · ·

In a chapter from *Random Memories* called "Rosa Quo Locorum" (from Horace: "the late rose fades"), Stevenson remembered when he first knew he was a reader. "I was sent into the village on an errand; and, taking a book of fairy tales, went down alone through a fir-wood, reading as I walked. How often since then has it befallen me to be happy even so; but that was the first time: the shock of that pleasure I have never since forgot, and if my mind serves me to the last, I never shall; for it was then I knew I loved reading."[5] Stevenson was a different reader at different times of his life. The "shock of pleasure" he experienced as a boy developed into an addiction when he got older. "I read now, yes, and with pleasure," he wrote when he was forty-one, "but some years ago I read with the greed and gusto of a pig, sucking up some of the very paper (you would think) into my brain." Stevenson thought reading hungrily "is the only kind of reading for which it is worth while to support the pains of writing."[6] Although he often read when he was confined to a sickbed, he could make a mental, sedentary activity sound visceral and athletic. "In anything fit to be called by the name of reading, the process itself should be absorbing and voluptuous; we should gloat over a book, be rapt clean out of ourselves, and rise from the perusal, our mind filled with the busiest, kaleidoscopic dance of images, incapable of sleep or of continuous thought."[7] This kind of reading is pure, gluttonous bliss and Stevenson made no apologies for it. It was this kind of experience that made him treasure certain books and return to them again and again. It was how he wished his own books to be read: he wanted to "make the reader eat and drink and breathe it."[8] You could say he wrote the kind of novels that he wanted to read, although once he finished writing a book it was impossible

· · · · · ·

to read it disinterestedly. "I have always thought it was one of the hardest parts of the fate of the man of letters that he has so few books he can read," he wrote to the young J. M. Barrie. "But there is the trouble—we cannot read our own books, and there are at least two of mine" (*Treasure Island* and *Kidnapped*) "that I would give thirty shillings to be able to peruse, for I have an idea they would amuse me."[9]

Although Stevenson never, ever stopped reading, when he was in his forties and living in Samoa, he missed the capacity to read with the kind of devouring appetite he used to have. He said that he wanted only to write books now "for the appreciation of the young," people who *needed* to read.[10] He was mentally restless and frustrated with the state of contemporary letters. "Small is the word; it is a small age, and I am of it," he wrote to Will Low. "Here is a long while I have been waiting for something *good* in art."[11] The "tepid feeling for literature," he wrote to another young author, "which is all that is left of my old ardour, makes me envious of my old experiences."[12] Readers of a certain age will understand his chagrin. A relationship with books can become a central part of who someone is, an instrumental aid in structuring an inner life. Being a reader was as much a part of Stevenson's self-identity as being a writer. When he agreed to contribute to a magazine series on the topic "Books Which Have Influenced Me," he wondered that a query so seemingly innocent could cut so deeply. He found with some dismay that he was engaged "upon a chapter in the life of that little, beautiful brother whom we once all had, and whom we have all lost and mourned, the man we ought to have been, the man we hoped to be."[13] To look back on our reading life is to revisit our own emotional and moral history, our sense of ourselves as it has evolved through the years. Stevenson's bookshelves were a tangible record of his aspirations and his delights—as well as his disappointments and his failures.

In the nineteenth century, the trope of wandering or adventuring through the world of books was commonplace, as was the idea of books as friends and companions. Stevenson liked to call himself "a literary vagrant."[14] And it was natural for a man as matey as RLS to consider reading as a test of friendship between author and reader, an enterprise both tentative and hopeful. Just as with our choice of friends, the authors we gravitate toward are a matter of taste, necessity, and personal inclination. "Not all men can read all books," Stevenson confessed. "[I]t is only in a chosen few that any man will find his appointed food."[15] When we find an author who meets our way of thinking and expression, it can feel like finding a soulmate. Love is not too strong a word. In some books—the *Meditations* of Marcus Aurelius, for example—"you carry away with you a memory of the man himself; it is as though you had touched a loyal hand, looked into brave eyes, and made a noble friend."[16] Not only authors but characters, too, could feel like companions: "Not even my friends are quite so real," he confessed, "perhaps quite so dear, as d'Artagnan," the hero of Dumas's *Three Musketeers* and *The Vicomte of Bragelonne*.[17] Fictional people can become moral guides. "I shall be very sorry for the man who is so much of a pedant in morals that he cannot learn from the Captain of Musketeers." "Few living friends have had upon me an influence so strong for good as Hamlet or Rosalind."[18] There are books that become part of a life's story. Stevenson would be the first to admit that his approach to life would have been decidedly diminished without the acquaintance of the clever d'Artagnan.

Stevenson thought a reader had to temporarily surrender to the author's imagined world, even if it's an uncomfortable place to be. After reading Dostoevsky in a French translation, he wrote to John Symonds,

> [*Crime and Punishment*] is the greatest book I have read easily in ten years.... Many find it dull; Henry James could not finish it: all I can say is it nearly finished me. It was like having an illness. James did

......

not care for it because the character of Raskolnikoff was not objective; and at that I divined a great gulf between us and, on further reflection, the existence of a certain impotence in many minds of today, which prevents them from living *in* a book or a character, and keeps them standing afar off, spectators of a puppet show. To such I suppose the book may seem empty in the centre; to the others it is a room, a house of life, into which they themselves enter, and are tortured and purified.[19]

Stevenson eminently possessed this capacity to live *in* a book. He had in abundance what he called "the gift of reading." Simply processing language—reading like a hog—is not the gift of reading. Even a reader who has been naively swept into the world of a novel and who completely identifies with the hero or heroine has not the gift. This kind of reader "migrates into such characters for the time of reading; under their name escapes the narrow prison of the individual career, and sates his avidity for other lives." Well and good. But it's not certain to "what extent he ever emigrates again, and how far the fancied careers react upon the true one."[20] To read without that reaction upon real life, to skip the process of reflection and speculation was how avid consumers of the Victorian penny press tended to read. They kept the publishing mill grinding away, but they were not *readers* in Stevenson's conception of the word.

In "Popular Authors," Stevenson tells a story about being on an emigrant ship in the Atlantic and asking a seaman experienced with all things ship-like if there was any book that gave a true picture of the sailor's life. The man thoughtfully recommended a popular novel called *Tom Holt's Log*, which Stevenson duly acquired. *Tom Holt's Log*, he recorded, had its merits, but the story was on the whole so outlandish, "now tedious, now extravagant—always acutely untrue to life as it is, often pleasantly coincident with childish hopes of what life ought to be," that Stevenson was as-

tonished that "this was the work that an actual tarry seaman recommended for a picture of his own existence!"[21]
Remembering his own youthful lust for the weekly gallery
of tales advertised in the stationer's window in Leith ("The
Baronet Unmasked," "So and So Approaching the Mysterious House," "The Discovery of the Dead Body in the Blue
Marl Pit," "Dr. Vargas Removing the Senseless Body of Fair
Lilias") and no doubt his own contributions to penny magazines such as *Young Folks*, Stevenson wondered, without a
bit of condescension, what goes on in the minds of adult
readers such as this seaman. Why are *Tom Holt's Log: A Tale
of the Deep Sea*, by STEPHENS HAYWARD (Stevenson put
the authors' names in capitals as a gesture of respect), and
The Bondage of Brandon, by BRACEBRIDGE HEMMING
so extremely popular?

The case of his sailor showed the grave importance of this
question for Stevenson, who lived during a time of explo-
sive mass readership—not only shilling shockers and penny
dreadfuls, but completely new genres: detective stories
(Arthur Conan Doyle, fellow Edinburgher), imperial adventure tales (H. Rider Haggard), fantasies and historical
romances (Marie Corelli, Lucas Malet, and Ouida), New
Woman novels (Sarah Grand and Mona Caird), and science
fiction (the young H. G. Wells). A lot of this fiction powerfully tapped into men's and women's fantasies and so potentially shaped their relation to reality and to their idea of
themselves. Popular novels, Stevenson observed, "were not
true to what men see; they were true to what the readers
dreamed." Stevenson's sailor sounds like a sketch for the
protagonist of Conrad's *Lord Jim*. He "lives surrounded by
the fact, and does not observe it. He cannot realise, he cannot make a tale of his own life; which crumbles in discrete
impressions even as he lives it, and slips between the fingers of his memory like sand. It is not this that he considers
in his rare hours of rumination, but that other life, which
was all lit up for him by the humble talent of a Hayward—

that other life which, God knows, perhaps he still believes that he is leading—the life of Tom Holt." Readers like this don't choose a book in order to expand their understanding. They want literature that will replay their desires over and over, with slight variations. Popular novelists conduct the "mighty public" where they wish to go in their fantasies. But it must, consistently, be where the reader has gone before—"That's the point; elsewhere they will not follow." "They long, not to enter into the lives of others, but to behold themselves in changed situations, ardently but impotently preconceived."[22] Impotently, because there's no moral or intellectual movement from author to book to reader to world. It's reading as quicksand.

Stevenson expected incredulous, optimistic readers to tell him that his seaman on the Atlantic liner was an exception to the rule, that most people don't read in that naive way. But Stevenson was "tempted to think, on the other hand, that he may be normal," and wondered if "the critical attitude, whether to books or life—how if that were the true exception?"[23] The critical attitude means a reader doesn't choose a book in order to disappear into his private fantasies or to confirm and bolster his private prejudices—at least, not as a regular thing. The beauty of novels is that they "disengage us from ourselves, they constrain us to the acquaintance of others; and they show us the web of experience, not as we can see it for ourselves, but with a singular change— that monstrous, consuming *ego* of ours being, for the nonce, struck out."[24] This is perhaps the best, most succinct explanation for the ethical effects of literary reading that anyone has devised. Stevenson thought that reading intelligently required self-vigilance as well as absorption. It's a two-way transaction. With the "genuine reader," he says, the author's words are not swallowed whole but are "weighed and winnowed, and only that which suits will be assimilated."[25] Active readers, who both exercise their judgment and meet the author halfway, are the best readers—and every author (except, perhaps, STEPHENS HAYWARD and company) hopes and prays for this kind of reader. For then the reader is a cointerpreter and cocreator of the book. But when an author's words "fall into the hands of one who cannot intelligently read," Stevenson maintained, "they come there quite silent and inarticulate, falling upon deaf ears, and his secret is kept as if he had not written."[26]

A critical reader is not the same as a literary critic, but Stevenson, of course, was also an exemplary critic, shrewd, generous, honest. His essays on Whitman, Thoreau, Hugo, Burns, and Samuel Pepys are well worth reading today. Stevenson could keep both sides of his reading experience, the personal and the objective, the immersive and the evaluative, in fine equilibrium—a difficult thing to do. He wondered about his two-sidedness in the preface to *Familiar Studies of Men and Books*: "For these were all men whom, for one reason or another, I loved; or when I did not love the men, my love was the greater to their books. I had read them and lived with them; for months they were continually in my thoughts; I seemed to rejoice in their joys and to sorrow with them in their griefs; and behold, when I came to write of them, my tone was sometimes hardly courteous and seldom wholly just."[27] Such is the duplicity—or the complete professionalism—of the literary critic. Stevenson, who devoured books like a beast and inhaled stories as if for life, concluded that reading required more than surrendering to an appetite. Reading also demanded a kind of restraint. Reading needs a sense of humility and a liberality of thought. When someone possesses together strong emotional responsiveness and mental discipline, that person may be said to have the gift of reading. It is, Stevenson offered, "not very common, nor very generally understood. It consists, first of all, in a vast intellectual endowment—a free grace, I find I must call it—by which a man rises to understand that he is not punctually right, nor those from whom he differs absolutely wrong." Grace and open-mindedness are the touchstones. "Something that seems quite new, or that seems insolently false or very dangerous, is the test of a reader. If he tries to see what it means, what truth excuses it, he has the gift, and let him read. If he is merely hurt, or offended, or exclaims upon his author's folly, he had better take to the daily papers; he will never be a reader."[28]

TRUTH

. . . .

The "happy star of this trade of writing is that it should combine pleasure and profit to both parties, and be at once agreeable, like fiddling, and useful, like good preaching."[1] The writer has a high calling. His work is not only to please, but to improve and instruct. Stevenson believed all forms of writing implicitly communicate the beliefs and values of their author and that writers can be important moral teachers. "There is no quite good book," he wrote in his essay on Dumas, "without a good morality."[2]

More than music, painting, or sculpture, literature has the potential to shape people's beliefs because "the material in which the literary artist works is the dialect of life."[3] Not everyone can handle a brush or play the violin, but everyone uses language. So literary works, from the humblest to the greatest, come home "easily and powerfully to the minds of men." And then literature drags with a wide net. No subject is closed to a writer, no form of expression prohibited. Novels, stories, poems, essays, and journalism have the capacity to reach many people, to form their thoughts and expand their perspectives. The writer is in a position "to build up the sum of sentiments and appreciations which goes by the name of Public Opinion or Public Feeling." "Any literary work which conveys faithful facts or pleasing impressions is a service to the public. . . . Every article, every piece of verse, every essay . . . is destined to pass, however swiftly, through the minds of some portion of the public, and to colour, however transiently, their thoughts." Stevenson believed writers could potentially wield considerable influence. "I still contend that, in the humblest sort of literary work, we have it in our power either to do great harm or great good."[4]

Stevenson came of age a generation after the big writers of the High Victorian period, men and women who earnestly believed that the mission of art and literature was to morally strengthen and ennoble people. Browning and Tennyson in poetry, Ruskin and Carlyle in prose, and in fiction Thackeray, Eliot, Trollope, the Brontës, and, of course, Dickens—these were towering names for would-be authors in the 1880s. Stevenson honored and admired them, and they shaped his comprehension of the writer's moral responsibilities. But he could not accept their authority unquestioningly, and as a writer he had no desire to duplicate their achievements. Dickens died in 1870 and George Eliot in 1880. The last two decades of the century felt looser— more exploratory and less rule-bound. Like many young artists and intellectuals of the fin de siècle, Stevenson did not want to tread the old road of triple-decker novels, angelic heroines, wrap-up endings, and narrative omniscience. Nor did he want to conform to conventional ideas about life, literature, love, or religion. To thoughtful, forward-looking men and women of his generation, independent thought and fearless self-creation were moral imperatives.

Stevenson fought hard to be true to himself. When he was in his twenties, in letter after letter, he defended his departure from his father's religious faith in terms of spiritual and intellectual integrity. "People must be themselves," he insisted.[5] To his cousin Bob he complained,

> It is all very well to talk about flesh and lusts and
> such like; but the real hot sweat must come out in this
> business, or we go alone to the end of life. *I* want an
> object, a mission, a belief, a hope to be my wife; and,
> please God, have it I shall.... It would be much easier to
> give over the pursuit, to leave the windy hunting ground

and go home to the warm ingle, to bid adieu to honesty and settle back to the old outward conformity; but I am damned if I don't carry it through.[6]

Stevenson knew that healthy self-love and brave self-scrutiny were vital for a creative person. Artists have to get to the marrow of who they are. The author of *Dr. Jekyll and Mr. Hyde* knew that if a writer can't be bothered to discover the good and the evil within himself, he probably should try another occupation. And a writer has to be a little egotistical, otherwise he wouldn't bother to publish anything. Stevenson confessed to one young writer, "I am a rogue at egotism myself and to be plain, I have rarely or never liked any man who was not. The first step to discovering the beauties of God's universe is usually a (perhaps partial) apprehension of such of them as adorn our own characters. When I see a man who does not think pretty well of himself, I always suspect him of being in the right."[7] He liked a bit of self-display in a writer. He called Samuel Pepys a "human-hearted egotist," whose remarkable Diary, unquestionably a work of literary art in Stevenson's view, was "worthy of prolonged and patient study."[8] He respected the self-importance of Whitman, "hymning the *ego* and commercing with God and the universe."[9] He took the essays of Montaigne as his models — glorious Montaigne, who wrote, "I am myself the matter of my book."[10]

Stevenson didn't care for moral busybodies or the virtue police. "There is an idea abroad among moral people that they should make their neighbours good. One person I have to make good: myself." People preach "noble self-denial" but self-sacrifice is nothing to admire if it brings anyone bitterness or misery.[11] He learned as a young writer that no genuine work of art can be conceived without integrity and a desire to approach the truth. Success without sincerity is a Faustian contract. This is not high-minded morality, but marketplace ethics. On one occasion, for example, Stevenson refused to accept the contractual amount of forty pounds for work he felt was not up to par. His friend W. E. Henley, an author and editor himself, thought he was utterly mad. Stevenson replied with some heat: "Are we artists or city men? Why do we sneer at stockbrokers? O nary; I will not take the £40. I took that as a fair price for my best work; I was not able to produce my best; and I will be damned if I steal with my eyes open.... If this is the honesty of authors—to take what you can get and console yourself because publishers are rich—take my name from the rolls of that association. 'Tis a caucus of weaker thieves, jealous of the stronger."[12]

To sacrifice honesty, even in the name of Art, was to Stevenson a form of self-betrayal. And dishonesty will make the work suffer in the long run. "In this strange welter where we live, all hangs together by a million filaments," he wrote to Low, "and to do reasonably well by others, is the first prerequisite of Art.... Art is a virtue; and if I were the man I should be, my art would rise in the proportion of my life."[13] Therefore know thyself. "Some part of the writer or his life will crop out in even a vapid book."[14] It is inevitably so. "The sum of virtue in our books is in a relation of equality to the sum of virtue in ourselves," he remarked to Theodore Watts-Dunton. To Henley he insisted, "Every defect in a man's character must out in his works."[15] I'm tempted to say that Stevenson wanted to be a good person in order to be a great writer.

A writer must tell the truth as he sees it. Nothing is more vital than sincerity. "Man is imperfect; yet, in his literature, he must express himself and his own views and preferences; for to do anything else is to do a far more perilous thing than to risk being immoral: it is to be sure of being untrue. To ape a sentiment, even a good one, is to travesty a sentiment; that will not be helpful. To conceal a sentiment, if you are sure you hold it, is to take a liberty with truth."[16] Yet to tell the truth about anything is formidably difficult, for "it has first to be discovered, and then justly and exactly uttered."[17] In the essay "Truth of Intercourse," Stevenson declared that an author's greatest challenge is to define his experience of life for himself, and then to describe it truthfully to another. "There are two distinct duties incumbent on any man who enters on the business of writing: truth to the fact and a good spirit in the treatment." An author's positive effort toward truth will be made manifest to a careful reader, even if the book is full of flaws. Even if "the main design be trivial or base," when the writer sincerely has something to say, some truth and beauty will be there. We know what Stevenson thought of the French realists. Yet he admitted that important truths can emerge even if an author's method is unnecessarily grimy. "When Flaubert wrote *Madame Bovary*, I believe he thought chiefly of a somewhat morbid realism; and behold! the book turned in his hands into a masterpiece of appalling morality."[18]

Stevenson said that no book is perfect because no person is. One man's pleasure is another's vice. "There is no quite good book without a good morality" is nicely epigrammatic, but the second half of the sentence is, "but the world is wide, and so are morals."[19] No one morality will serve every reader. So what readers inevitably take away from a book is *not* a set of moral instructions. They take the writer's attitude, which can amount to "a whole experience and a theory of life."[20] Yet even this most essential communication is bound to be incomplete. "Every one who lives any semblance of an inner life thinks more nobly and profoundly than he speaks; and the best of teachers can impart only broken images of the truth which they perceive." An author's insight is infinitely deferred because "true knowledge is eternally incommunicable, for it is a knowledge of himself."[21] Everyone has been influenced by Wordsworth's poetry, Stevenson observed, but no one can tell precisely how the poems have worked on his sensibility. "I do not know that you learn a lesson; you need not ... agree with any one of his beliefs; and yet the spell is cast. Such are the best teachers; a dogma learned is only a new error—the old one was perhaps as good; but a spirit communicated is a perpetual possession. These best teachers climb beyond teaching to the plane of art; it is themselves, and what is best in themselves, that they communicate."[22]

The moral intelligence behind a novel or poem and the spirit in which it was written were the most important things to Stevenson—much, much more important than an author's subject matter or style. In a review comparing Stevenson to Sir Walter Scott, Edward Purcell observed that Scott, who lived through a comparatively stable period of history, had a mind that was made up about life, whereas Stevenson, product of a troubled, modern age, could not help but express "doubt and difficulty."[23] Stevenson wrote to Purcell,

> For God's sake, dear sir, do not compare me to Scott....
> I know Scott's novels to be full of sawdust, but they are
> full besides of organic blood, and built for posterity...
> and I think the difference lies deeper, far deeper, than
> your kind humour led you to indicate. It lies in the
> genius, human, quiet, solid, smiling, unperturbed, of Sir
> Walter; not in changing phases of opinion. It lies also ...
> in the fact that Sir Walter was a good man, and a good
> man content with a more or less conventional solution,
> whereas I am only a man who would be content to be
> good if I knew what goodness was—and could lay hold
> of it.[24]

Stevenson's essay on the poet Robert Burns finely expressed his ideas about art and morality. Burns, as was well known, was quite fond of the bonnie lassies. As Stevenson put it, he had "no very elegant reputation as to morals." After his blazing success as the ploughman poet in 1786, Burns went rapidly downhill. "He lost his habits of industry and formed the habit of pleasure." In an effort to do his duty, he made a disastrous marriage. He was, observed Stevenson, "equally at the call of his worse and better instincts," not cruel enough to be a real Don Juan but not strong enough to resist his impulses. He had lost his way, he had fallen, and he had failed. "Drink and debauchery" became "the means of his unconscious suicide."[25] Burns died in his thirty-seventh year.

Burns saw into his own nature very clearly and very painfully. His letters proved this uncontestably, said Stevenson. He could read other people like a book, but "what is yet more rare, his knowledge of himself equalled his knowledge of others." Burns "had none of that blind vanity which values itself on what it is not; he knew his own strength and weakness to a hair: he took himself boldly for what he was, and ... declared himself content."[26] Burns's own summing up, his sadness and bewilderment at his inability to conquer his nature and be a better man, drew Stevenson's pity and esteem. In his preface to *Familiar Studies of Men and Books*, Stevenson expressed his indignation at "the common, trashy mind of our generation" that could reduce Robert Burns to "an impure vehicle of fine verses." Anyone with a soul should see that Burns "shines out tenfold more nobly in the failure of that frantic effort to do right, than if he had ... married a congenial spouse, and lived orderly, and died reputably an old man."[27] To miss the beauty of that effort was to apply the narrowest morality.

No one among these prigs and philistines dared deny that Burns's early poems were great. His verse changed the course of English literature. But the importance of Burns wasn't his choice of "homely subject matter." After all, he was a peasant farmer; he didn't exactly choose his subjects according to poetic principles. Burns influenced other poets, Stevenson argued, because his lyric voice was fresh, honest, and transparently generous. Burns's poems "interest us not in themselves, but because they have been passed through the spirit of so genuine and vigorous a man." What touched Stevenson's compassion and admiration was just that Burns was Burns, and his poetry is inescapably stamped with his affections and his flaws. "What a gust of sympathy there is in him," Stevenson said, "sometimes flowing out in byways hitherto unused, upon mice, and flowers, and the devil himself." "He loved to force his personality upon the world. He would please himself, and shine." When he crashed, he paid the rueful penalty down to the last farthing. "He died of being Robert Burns," Stevenson concluded, "and there is no levity in such a statement of the case; for shall we not, one and all, deserve a similar epitaph?"[28]

Burns's failure interested Stevenson as much, if not more, than his brief success or his lasting fame. For the inevitability of failure became the bedrock of Stevenson's philosophy, about writing and about life. "There is indeed one element in human destiny that not blindness itself can controvert: whatever else we are intended to do, we are not intended to succeed; failure is the fate allotted. It is so in every art and study; it is so above all in the continent art of living well."[29] Trying to be decent, doing a thing honestly, cultivating one's character—this mattered so much more than the outcome of one's choices, which, if you take the long view, are beyond what anyone can foretell. This idea is expressed chillingly in "Markheim," one of Stevenson's best short stories, his homage to Dostoevsky. Even a bad act, says the mysterious stranger in the tale, if followed "far enough down the hurtling cataract of the ages, might yet be found more blessed than those of the rarest virtues."[30] At the cusp of thirty, Stevenson wrote to Henley,

> I'll be a good man, I'll grow better every day, or be damned. I think I have little to be sorry for, when I look widely. I fight the fight. If people knew all that was in my mind, they would know *me* at least, and know

besides that I have parted company with half of man and nearly half of myself. I'm not good, but I'm trying. If we all were, it would be a happy world. We don't want to succeed; success is a part of fortune, and a small thing both to the world and the individual. After all what he was trying for, was a mistake; if he succeeded, as they call it, his success would trail a thousand evils in its following; it is his trying that is the true success. We are not trying to succeed, but trying to try. I have not been useless. I have given love and friendship. I have tried. I have lived a life.[31]

Although this letter sounds as if Stevenson needed to convince himself that he didn't care about success, he was expressing a profound truth and a philosophy he never lost sight of. Though RLS was as devoted to the study of literature as any writer of his age, he also knew that his choice of a career was just a part of his life, not the whole of it. "Books are good enough in their own way, but they are a mighty bloodless substitute for life," he wrote in one essay. "It seems a pity to sit, like the Lady of Shalott, peering into a mirror, with your back turned on all the bustle and glamour of reality. And if a man reads very hard, as the old anecdote reminds us, he will have little time for thought."[32] He confessed in a letter of 1886 that he was "a person who prefers life to art, and who knows it is a far finer thing to be in love, or to risk a danger, than to paint the finest picture or write the noblest book."[33] Stevenson would never ask a writer to sacrifice truth, generosity of mind, loving kindness, or a sense of personal duty to achieve literary success. "God keep me brave and singleminded; God help me to kind words and actions; what more is there to pray for?" he continued in the letter to Henley. He cherished his art, and he felt that books and writing had literally saved his life. But for all his devotion to craft and to style, Stevenson's fundamental advice to authors was moral advice. "Everything but prejudice should find a voice through him; he should see the good in all things; where he has even a fear that he does not wholly understand, there he should be wholly silent. He should recognise from the first that he has only one tool in his workshop, and that tool is sympathy."[34]

TEACHING

. . . .

"**B**urns would have been no Scotchman," wrote one of the poet's biographers, "if he had not loved to moralise."[1] Stevenson was delighted with this observation, for it excused his own penchant to step up to the pulpit. In his letters, of course, he pontificated magnificently. But he also recognized early in his career the opportunities of the essay form as a vehicle for his inner preacher, and by the time he reached his thirties, Stevenson had developed a reputation as a superb essayist.

Stevenson's openness and his welcoming, familiar voice became his signature traits, both as a writer and a public figure. Readers who felt such intimacy with his authorial persona were pleasantly surprised to find that Stevenson was pretty much the same in person as in print. Many of his acquaintances noted this. "I never learned to love a man so much in so short a time," wrote Edward Eggleston. "He had no fences. He had no secrecy. He gave me out of his heart. . . . His was a sweet personality—a singularly unveiled soul. There were no hedges about him."[2] An American reporter wrote, "Mr. Stevenson's talk is very like his writing; it is fresh, racy, redolent of the soil out of which he has grown. . . . He sees everything from his own point of view, and puts his case, not dogmatically, but pictorially, graphically, with pith and force of a perfectly direct and sincere nature."[3] Stevenson wrote with the earnestness and warmth of a man who was eager for *a good talk*; and in the essay, "On Talk and Talkers," he made patent the relationship between the art of writing and the art of conversation: "Literature in many of its branches is no other than the shadow of good talk."[4]

Many readers enjoyed being welcomed into so relaxed a conversation. As one reviewer periphrastically put it, "To accept his invitation will be a refreshment to every one who can enjoy holding conversation on the daily and vital facts of life with a writer who, accepting nothing second-hand, brings to bear on the facts of experience a gift of singularly luminous and genial insight, and perception both poignant and picturesque."[5] William Archer struck the same note more succinctly: "As a rule, Mr. Stevenson gossips along as lightly as need be. His is healthy human speech, sane and self-contained. We can listen to it long without either irritation or tedium." There were some, of course, who did begin to yawn at Mr. Stevenson's cheerful commentaries on how to live. It wasn't just the moralizing that irked them. They grew tired of Stevenson's chumminess, his extremely subjective turn of mind—his "ever-present self-consciousness," as Archer put it.[6] "Mr. Stevenson's essays positively bristle with 'you see,' 'you remember,' 'I say,' 'I fancy,' and the rest of it," wrote George Saintsbury.[7] "Do, my good Sir," he protested, "leave my buttons alone." Being grasped, however lightly, by the lapels is not to everyone's taste.

Others expressed strong reservations about the meaningfulness and depth of Stevenson's chitchat. Archer's praise was heavily qualified: "We can listen to it long without either irritation or tedium, until suddenly there vibrates across our memory an echo of some other utterance compared with which this light-flowing discourse 'is as moonlight unto sunlight, is as water unto wine.'" RLS, wrote Archer, has "a vague way of alluding to some esoteric morality of his own, which is as impressive as it is tantalizing. . . . This nebulous cocksureness, this dogmatism without dogma, at last becomes a little irritating." He called Stevenson "a humourist and an artist in words" with no concept of "the life of pain, and terror, and weariness, into which it is part of his philosophy to look as seldom as possible." Archer felt there must be a time for everything. We sometimes need power and passion and a more solemn tone; we cannot always be happy pagans seeking our pleasure. He thus objected to the "commonplace optimism" implied in Stevenson's conversational style, and complained that his "athletico-aesthetic" bearing quickly became cloying and tiresome to sober adults. Is it a responsible philosophy of life, Archer wondered, to reject logic and objective discourse and place one's trust in something called "the heart," or something even vaguer called "the eyes and the sympathies and appetites," as Mr. Stevenson would have us do? Mr. Archer thought not.[8]

And it was not only Mr. Archer who murmured. Other critics who acknowledged Stevenson's style, his charm, his buoyancy were quite ready to bash his immaturity and the simplicity of his thought. The Irish writer George Moore dismissed Stevenson's "conception of life" as "trivial . . . never higher than that of a blithe, noble-hearted boy." His famous "style," said Moore, was just a trick, and the public fell for it. Henry Purcell (who never liked Stevenson) referred to his "puzzling, enigmatic ethics." "Stevenson had not—he never will have—any gospel of life to give us." For fellow Scotsman J. M. Barrie, RLS was "a warm, genial writer" with absolutely no interest in "the affairs of life and death on which other minds are chiefly set. . . . His philosophy is that we are but as the light-hearted birds." "He never grew up," according to John Jay Chapman. "Whether or not there was some obscure connection between his bodily troubles and the arrest of his intellectual development, it is certain that Stevenson remained a boy till the day of his death."[9]

The stigma that he "wrote with the brain of a boy" clung to Stevenson's reputation for decades.[10] He was "the Peter Pan of Samoa."[11] Even G. K. Chesterton, who after Stevenson's death rushed to defend his work against negative appraisements, felt compelled to refer to "the splendidly infantile character of Stevenson's mind."[12] RLS entertained wondrously, and he had many gifts as a writer. Everyone agreed to that. But it seemed he had no wisdom to impart, nothing serious to teach people. "When we come to look at Mr. Stevenson as a teacher," wrote Archer, "we find that, in his case, at least, the style is the man himself ... for is not the ever-recurring burden of Mr. Stevenson's wisdom an exhortation to cultivate lightness of touch upon the chords of life?"[13]

Stevenson was upset by Archer's article, especially, he said, "the attacks on my morality." He initiated a correspondence in which he defended his development as a writer: "You take my young books as my last word.... And you make no allowance for the slowness with which a man finds and tries to learn his tools. I began with a neat brisk little style, and a sharp little knack for partial observation: I have tried to expand my means, but still I can utter only a part of what I wish to say, and am bound to feel; and much of it will die unspoken."[14] He corrected the impression that RLS was a robust man with a robust philosophy: "To me, the medicine bottles on my chimney and the blood on my handkerchief are accidents; they do not colour my view of life .... I would as soon drag them under the eyes of readers as I would mention a pimple I might chance to have (saving your presence) on my bottom." And he described a fundamental difference in their worldviews: "And here we come to the division: not only do I believe that literature should give joy, but I see a universe, I suppose, eternally different from yours: a solemn, a terrible but a very joyous and noble universe; where suffering is not at least wantonly inflicted, though it falls with dispassionate partiality, but where it may be and generally is nobly borne; where, above all, *any brave man may make* out a life which shall be happy for himself and, by so being, beneficent [*sic*] to those about him." Stevenson said plainly that "morals, the conscience, the affections, and the passions are, I will own frankly and sweepingly, so infinitely more important than the other parts of life that I conceive men rather triflers who become immersed in the latter."[15]

We think we have seen a fleeting truth about the world, and the next moment something happens that calls everything we believed into question. Is there any ground to stand on? "We have no more than glimpses and touches; we are torn away from our theories; we are spun round and round and shown this or the other view of life, until only fools or knaves can hold to their opinions." We're not even the same person from one day to the next. "And we cannot even regard ourselves as a constant; in this flux of things, our identity itself seems in a perpetual variation; and not infrequently we find our own disguise the strangest in the masquerade." We desire consistency, we aim for the bull's eye, we follow the thread to the middle of the maze. But, Stevenson asked, "How if there were no centre at all, but just one alley after another, and the whole world a labyrinth without end or issue?"[16] Where do we get our morals from then? Who is there to guide us?

Critics who questioned Stevenson's moral seriousness or objected to his jauntiness—a minority, but a vocal minority—must have skipped essays such as "Pulvis et Umbra," "Pan's Pipes," "A Christmas Sermon," "Crabbed Age and Youth," "Aes Triplex," "El Dorado," and even "Ordered South." Some people have called him a stoic, and certainly he had great admiration for the lessons of Marcus Aurelius. Yet I see a nearer affinity with some of the teachings of Buddhism. By the 1880s, Buddhist texts had made their way to the West. Traces of Buddhist thought can be found in different discourses from the period, from popular fiction to psychology to spiritualism. To see the world and the self in flux, to accept that nothing is permanent and that life is suffering, to make bravery, gratitude, and joy daily practices, to know that sympathy is the greater part of wisdom: these concepts seem wholly built into Stevenson's outlook and his way of being in the world.

......

His thoughts about teaching, too, had a Buddhist slant. Eve Sedgwick has described Buddhist pedagogy as "an exchange of recognition—at best, surprising recognition." Inside the pupil there is already a shadowy template of knowledge, which can be clarified only by an encounter that he apprehends as "true" because (as in the brand name of a popular Buddhist audiotape) it *sounds true*. "By the criterion of 'sounds true,' one can apparently learn only what one already knows."[17] This special kind of learning is beyond mere argument. It appeals to something ineffable, a place deep within, a buried responsiveness. Our emotions may be awakened by both everyday and rare experiences—the beauty of a sunset, the flight of a kestrel. Something melancholy may touch us when we watch the waves wash in and out on the shore, or we may feel a sudden excitement in catching sight of a galloping horse. This is the real stuff. A writer, said Stevenson, has to get at *those* kinds of responses. He has to "convince like nature, and not like books." How should he proceed? "Is there no actual piece of nature that he can show the man to his face, as he might show him a tree if they were walking together?" he asked in his essay on Whitman. "Yes, there is one: the man's own thoughts. In fact, if the poet is to speak efficaciously, he must say what is already in his hearer's mind. That, alone, the hearer will believe; that, alone, he will be able to apply intelligently to the facts of life."[18]

There is a Buddhist proverb: "When the student is ready, the teacher will appear." Teachers come to us in various guises. When a person reads a poem or a novel, there is always the possibility of a private communication. Everyone has a cherished corner of the self, a secret lantern carried inside his coat. In the essay "Lay Morals," Stevenson wrote about an "inner consciousness, this lantern alternately obscured and shining, to and by which the individual exists and must order his conduct," which "is something special to himself." "His joys delight, his sorrows wound him, according as *this* is interested or indifferent in the affair. . . . He may lose all, and *this* not suffer; he may lose what is materially a trifle and *this* leap in his bosom with a cruel pang. I do not speak of it to hardened theorists: the living man knows keenly what it is I mean."[19] Call it the soul or the conscience, it's "a central self," in Stevenson's words, not cognitive but intuitive knowledge, something deep down that's just *known*. A contemporary psychoanalyst, Christopher Bollas, has created the term *the unthought known* for this kind of understanding.[20] Stevenson called it an awareness of "a great and unqualified readiness." A religious person, he said, might see it as "the love of God," a Darwinian scientist as "an inherited . . . instinct to preserve self and propagate the race." "I am not, for the moment, averse to either theory, but it will save time to call it righteousness."[21] Whatever the name, it is the core awareness of movements afoot that are greater than oneself, but crucially and mysteriously involve oneself. It's the thing people hunger and thirst for. It's just *this*.

What is the purpose, then, of any kind of moral teaching, whether in art or in life? Stevenson answered, "To keep a man awake. To keep him alive to his own soul."[22] Then what is the method? It is to reveal to the student what he already knows; it is to show him himself. "He cannot be made to believe anything; but he can be made to see that he has always believed it. And this is the practical canon. It is when the reader cries, 'Oh, I know!'" (Sounds true!) "and is, perhaps, half irritated to see how nearly the author has forestalled his own thoughts, that he is on the way to what is called in theology a Saving Faith."[23] Teachers "must say what will remind the pupil of his soul; . . . must speak that soul's dialect; . . . must talk of life and conduct as his soul would have him think of them." Rather than drumming his own knowledge or his own creed into a student, a true teacher has to say "anything that [a student] has once thought, or been upon the point of thinking, or show him any view of life that he has once clearly seen, or been upon the point of clearly seeing." Then he has done his part and may leave the pupil "to complete the education for himself."[24]

In his essays, Stevenson's hidden didacticism offered, as Archer correctly observed, "some echo or semblance of a message," not a law or a blueprint.[25] He presented his thoughts in a roundabout way, through the pleasure of self-observation. The word *essay* means an *attempt*, a trying out of an idea. An essay is a riff, an experiment—Montaigne said, "I speak as an ignorant inquirer, referring the decision purely and simply to the common and authorized beliefs. I do not teach, I tell."[26] Stevenson's love of talk and his disingenuously titled "gossips" on various topics were polite refusals of pretentious or systematic argument. Like Montaigne, he didn't want to prove anything; he merely wanted to inquire, to see what he thought. He didn't even want the reader to be able to summarize what he had just read. He wanted to offer the reader an experience. His clean, friendly style and his determination to delight are ungraspable qualities, but they may set off ripples and resonances. Stevenson implicitly asked his readers to stop requiring explanations, to stop reading for clear-cut messages—to stop being overly attached learners. Like Wordsworth, he knew that we learn best when we are relaxed, when we expect pleasure, and when we are made happy. Stevenson's "lightness of touch" may have looked like irresponsible blitheness, but "to please is to serve," he reminded his critics, "and so far from its being difficult to instruct while you amuse, it is difficult to do the one thoroughly without the other."[27]

People do not change their lives because "the weapons of dialectic" are flashed before their eyes; "it is not by induction, deduction, or construction; it is not by forcing him on from one stage of reasoning to another, that the man will be effectually renewed."[28] Bland punditries and ideological platitudes won't touch the lineaments of knowledge that are waiting to become clear in a person's center. The creative artist has his own special door into people's *this*—and it's a back door. Stevenson cannot explain why all the labor a writer puts into his art should matter in the world, but he feels it does. "We may be sure (although we know not why) that we give our lives, like coral insects, to build up insensibly, in the twilight of the seas of time, the reef of righteousness. And we may be sure (although we know not how) it is a thing worth doing."[29] He said that the influence of books is "profound and silent, like the influence of nature; they mould by contact; we drink them up like water, and are bettered, yet know not how."[30] In a scientific and skeptical age, this not-knowing-how or not-knowing-why attitude must have sounded a bit fey. For Stevenson, it was a rope let down into the darkness, a small protest against officialdom and dogma. A profession of humanistic faith.

. . . . . .

"To travel hopefully is a better thing than to arrive and the true success is to labour." "I travel not to go anywhere, but to go. I travel for travel's sake." "The best that we find in our travels is an honest friend."[31] Websites devoted to inspirational quotes usually include dozens attributed to Stevenson.[32] To some, these aphorisms evoke RLS, the watery optimist, just as several books published in the early twentieth century evoked RLS, the sage of Skerryvore—*The Wisdom of Robert Louis Stevenson* (1904), *The Pocket R. L. S.* (1906), even *Brave Words about Death: From the Works of R. L. Stevenson* (1916).

I have to wonder what Stevenson would have thought of this posthumous branding. For when he tried to trace the lessons learned from his meanderings, he was confounded. There was no pearl of wisdom, no center to the labyrinth, because the lesson really *was*, for Stevenson, in the journey. He lived fortuitously and made no apology for chatting about whatever he encountered along the way. He possessed a rare and salient gift in a writer: he trusted himself. Henry

James wrote of Stevenson, "His feelings are always his reasons; he regards them, whatever they may be, as sufficiently honorable, does not disguise them in other names or colors." In his comfortable, noticing way, Stevenson's essays model what it might feel like to be conscious and free and awake. His essays were gestures toward the virtues he wished to attain himself: serenity, gratitude, courage, and high spirits. Do not complain, warned James, if you miss "the respectable, desirable moral which many a reader doubtless finds that [Mr. Stevenson] neglects to point."[33] That's mistaking the words for the thing, like the Buddhist sutra of the finger pointing at the moon. Do not get attached to the words! The words are necessary, but they are only the "broken images of the truth," as Stevenson put it, that the teacher internally perceives.[34] Gaze beyond the words, and you will recognize *this*, what as a living, warring, irradiating person you already know.

The phrase "it's all around you" is a familiar Buddhist teaching. In "An Apology for Idlers," Stevenson wrote, "There is certainly some chill and arid knowledge to be found upon the summits of formal and laborious science; but *it is all round about you*, and for the trouble of looking, that you will acquire the warm and palpitating facts of life."[35]

Sounds true.

STYLE

S tevenson's contemporaries in the literary world agreed that he had a striking literary style, but there wasn't always consensus on how to characterize it. Reviewers looked up and down for apt comparisons, veering from "over smart, well-dressed, shall I say, like a young man walking in the Burlington Arcade" to "the heaviness and sententiousness of John Knox's prelections" to "one among the many products of the Queen Anne revival." This last critic said, not without admiration, "Mr. Stevenson is a stylist who lays himself out for the mastery of style."[1] Some people thought he was a little show-offy, as though writing trimly and resonantly was part of his pose, like his long hair.

Stevenson never got around to publishing a book on style for writers, as he said he wanted to, but he did publish an essay on the subject, of which he was modestly proud. "On Some Technical Elements of Style in Literature" attempted to define what makes a good style and to direct authors, both in prose and verse, toward practical applications. Stevenson saw style as the interweaving of sound and sense, form and meaning. "The web, then, or the pattern: a web at once sensuous and logical, an elegant and pregnant texture: that is style, that is the foundation of the art of literature." He wrote a formal conclusion to the essay, in which he briefly enumerated "the elements of style." The author has "the task of keeping his phrases large, rhythmical, and pleasing to the ear, without ever allowing them to fall into the strictly metrical" and "the task of artfully combining the prime elements of language into phrases that shall be musical in the mouth."

Also, "the task of weaving their argument into a texture of committed phrases and of rounded periods," as well as "the task of choosing apt, explicit, and communicative words." It's a very difficult game, all of this weaving of textures and juggling of tasks. It's no wonder, he said, "if perfect sentences are rare, and perfect pages rarer." Yet he believed that with "industry and intellectual courage" any committed author could learn the basics of good style.[2]

"On Some Technical Elements of Style in Literature" would seem to be the place to start in a chapter on style. But it's a rather heavy-footed essay. One commentator asked drily, "How comes it, one would like to know, that the act of writing about style tends to play havoc with the style of the writer? Mr. Stevenson's essay on style . . . was probably the worst piece of writing he ever put his name to."[3] I could almost agree with him. It's not my favorite. There's a little too much of the professorial "we," as in "[w]e do not, indeed, find verses in six groups, because there is not room for six in the ten syllables." To get a *feel* for good style, it might be better to carefully read "The Lantern-Bearers" or "An Apology for Idlers" rather than "On Some Technical Elements of Style in Literature" (even the title is clunky).

And yet this essay, more than any other, testifies to Stevenson's almost wonky interest in language and its refinements, his expert's appreciation for good writing, and his keen eye and ear for inferior work. He often felt that the great stylists were all in the past—uncommon men, who could write novels and poetry while also working as magistrates (Fielding), booksellers (Richardson), and lawyers (Scott). "The little, artificial popularity of style in England tends, I think, to die out," Stevenson complained to Richard Le Gallienne. The British reader returns "to his true love, the love of the style-less, of the shapeless, of the slap-dash and the disorderly." Stevenson didn't like to see a writer's gifts being thrown away on popular trends or turned into journalism: in the letter to Le Gallienne, he went on to observe that

"Kipling, with all his genius ... is a move in that direction, and it is the wrong one."[4] To develop a style required intelligence and perseverance. The writer is a ringmaster who must make the animals—words, rhymes, images—dance to a pipe or jump through hoops. The animals are often unruly or lethargic. Words, especially, have an annoying habit of wandering off and generating meanings in all directions. They are like intractable building blocks manhandled every day by advertisers and lawyers and politicians. A writer must show great precision and sensitivity and "by the tact of application touch them to the finest meanings and distinctions, restore them to their primal energy."[5] The *primal energy* of words—maybe for RLS, they were less like circus animals than mythical, slippery creatures, a kind of primordial hydra. Writing is like lion-taming, then, or alchemy—or maybe midwifery. "A work of art is first cloudily conceived in the mind; during the period of gestation it stands more clearly forward from these swaddling mists, puts on expressive lineaments, and becomes at length that most faultless, but also, alas! that incommunicable product of the human mind, a perfected design."[6]

It's at this point, when the writer has the outline for his work ready in his mind, that the *artist* must become the *artisan*; he must put on his apron, pick up his chisel, and hammer out the scale, the style, the overall execution. For some writers this is the fun part. "The engendering idea of some works is stylistic; a technical preoccupation stands them instead of some robuster principle of life. And with these the execution is but play; for the stylistic problem is resolved beforehand, and all large originality of treatment wilfully foregone."[7] This approach to style is serviceable, but it's a shortcut, pre-planned and formulaic. For a preoccupation with style is not where a writer should begin at all. Works of art are "conceived from within outwards, and generously nourished from the author's mind." Far from being the easy thing, building up the architecture from mere words is usually the most difficult stage of the process, "one of extreme perplexity and strain." Some writers—those "of indifferent energy and an imperfect devotion to their own ideal"—prefer to nail down their style once and for all, to hit on a style and stick with it.[8] They'll cling to the raft they've built, avoid rocks and breakers, and glide safely to shore. The style will be tidy. The prose will be lifeless. It will sound like this:

> It is with sincere regret that we have to inform our readers that the publication of this story is discontinued from this date. It is never an agreeable duty to withhold a promised pleasure, but our readers will readily believe that we should not have broken off the story thus suddenly if we had not been forced to do so by circumstances which we need not describe in detail.

This delicious sample made Stevenson roar. He wrote to Gosse, "Dear Weg, If you are taking *Young Folks*, for God's Sake Twig the editorial style: it is incredible; we are all left PANTING IN THE REAR. Twig, O twig it. His name is Clinton; I should say the most melodious prose writer now alive; it's like buttermilk and blacking; it sings and hums away in that last sheet, like a great old kettle filled with bilge water." No harmony, no rhythm, no brightness—alas! too many there were like "the rhythmic Clinton."[9]

Stevenson gloried in salty, varicolored language, in clever combinations of words, in alliteration and the vernacular. His letters, like this one to Gosse—prankish, funny, figurative—suggest that it wasn't *style* the sedulous ape pursued with such devotion. It was *words*, skittish, swarming, pullulating words, in and out of the dictionary, archaic words, new words, foreign words, curse words, Scots words, slang words, puns. And his incessant reading gave him a copious vocabulary. Barry Menikoff has listed all the words from Stevenson's fiction that were in the original *OED* when it was being compiled in the late nineteenth century.[10] Today, the *OED* online cites R. L. Stevenson 2,174 times. There are many words where he is the only example listed, including *blue fear, clumped, ergotize, febricule, harlequinesque, ivory-faced, run-the-hedge, sea quags, whip-top*, and *withinsides*. In his letters, he liked to use nautical words, Latin exclamations, Scots words, Biblical-sounding phrases, and nonsense words—sometimes all in one sentence: "It is low, damp and *mauchy*; the rain it raineth every day; and the dam glass goes tol-de-rol-de-riddle."[11] Indeed, Stevenson's friend, the Scottish writer Andrew Lang, found it curious that "this purist had a boyish habit of slang."[12] Flora Masson records a visit to the Stevensons in which father and son heatedly debated word coinage.

> Mr. Stevenson upheld the doctrine of a 'well of English undefiled,' which of course made Louis Stevenson rattle off with extraordinary ingenuity whole sentences composed of words of foreign origin taken into our language from all parts of the world—words of the East, of classical Europe, of the West Indies, and modern American slang. By a string of sentences he proved the absurdity of such a doctrine, and indeed its practical impossibility. It was a real feat in the handling of language, and I can see to this day his look of pale triumph.[13]

It is, perhaps, not very startling to claim that a writer is passionately attached to the material he works in. Yet Stevenson had a feeling for words that verged on the mystical in their power to conjure images: *post-chaise* and *ostler* triggered cocked hats and old inns, *headers* and *string-course* evoked the mysteries of engineering. He liked musical and mouthful words, especially in the Scots he had his ear tuned to as a boy. The romance of Scots, that "illustrious and malleable tongue," that "very dark oracular medium," never left him; he regretted deeply that the language seemed to be dying out.[14] Because publishers of his Scottish fiction didn't want to alienate English and American readers, Stevenson often had to tone it down. Sometimes he got a little defensive. He wrote to Gosse,

> *English*, the, a dull people incapable of comprehending the Scottish tongue. Their history is so intimately connected with that of Scotland, that we must refer our readers to that heading. Their literature is principally the work of venal Scots.
> Stevenson's *Handy Cyclopœdia*; Glascow: Blaikie & Bannock.[15]

He let himself go only in his letters to fellow Scotsmen and in a handful of poems:

> *"What tongue does your auld bookie speak?"*
> He'll spier; an' I, his mou to steik:
> *"No bein' fit to write in Greek,*
> *I wrote in Lallan,*
> *Dear to my heart as the peat reek,*
> *Auld as Tantallon.["]*[16]

It may have been his experience with the Scots language that spurred Stevenson's interest in Samoan, which he learned to speak and to write, even though there existed at the time virtually no Samoan literature. It was a rich, beautiful language to him, both grammatically and aurally. He admired "the *finesse* of the pronouns," for instance, which he thought "exquisitely elegant, and make the mouth of the *littérateur* to water."[17] "O Colvin, what a tongue it would be to write, if one only knew it—and there were only readers. Its curse in common use is an incredible left-handed wordiness; but in the hands of a man like Pratt [a missionary who translated the Bible and some fables into Samoan] it is succinct as Latin, compact of long rolling polysyllables and little and often pithy particles, and for beauty of sound a dream."[18] This last remark was especially important, for Stevenson had a gifted ear. "None can care for literature in itself who do not take a special pleasure in the sound of names," he wrote. He relished the Indian names of the American states, which formed "a chorus of sweet and most romantic vocables."[19] He practically wrote love songs to the names of Scottish streams and rivers.

Comely sounds, rhythm in the sentence, balanced phrases, not too much repetition—these were the essentials. "Each phrase of each sentence, like an air or a recitative in music, should be so artfully compounded out of long and short, out of accented and unaccented, as to gratify the sensual ear." Style is largely a blending of *sounds*, an orchestration with varied instruments so that none dominates. "And of this the ear is the sole judge. It is impossible to lay down laws. Even in our accentual and rhythmic language no analysis can find the secret of the beauty of a verse; how much less, then, of those phrases, such as prose is built of, which obey no law but to be lawless and yet to please?" With enough practice, harmony becomes a habit. Writers learn to avoid what is harsh and to buttress a phrase with "a patch of assonance or a momentary jingle of alliteration." Just read some bad writing, Stevenson advised, to understand why good writers are constantly preoccupied with pacing and sound. "There, indeed, you will find cacophony supreme, the rattle of incongruous consonants only relieved by the jaw-breaking hiatus, and whole phrases not to be articulated by the powers of man."[20]

The skillful and accurate deployment of language penetrates every corner of human activity. Stevenson's stylistic advice applied not only to professional writers, but to all who used rhetoric to persuade or to communicate their meaning—and that would be just about everyone. "The difficulty of literature is not to write, but to write what you mean; not to affect your reader, but to affect him precisely as you wish."[21] People who see poems and novels as remote, arty things that really have nothing to do with getting up and going to work fail to comprehend the ubiquity of the literary in everyday human intercourse. "But one thing you can never make Philistine natures understand," Stevenson wrote, "one thing, which yet lies on the surface, remains as unseizable to their wits as a high flight of metaphysics — namely, that the business of life is mainly carried on by means of this difficult art of literature, and according to a man's proficiency in that art shall be the freedom and the fulness of his intercourse with other men."[22] An alert sense for the nuances of meaning, patient care for the beauty and strangeness of our language — these are hard qualities to develop and retain. But our relationships with other people depend largely on this sensitivity. "It is really a most delicate affair," he insisted. "The world was made before the English language, and seemingly upon a different design. Suppose we held our converse, not in words, but in music; those who have a bad ear would find themselves cut off from all near commerce, and no better than foreigners in this big world. But we do not consider how many have 'a bad ear' for words, nor how often the most eloquent find nothing to reply."[23]

Someone who has never written a line, though, may have quite a good ear, an instinct for repetitive or fluid sounds, alphabetical ordering, or the bon mot. In fact, many people do, without realizing it. A person may assume he's thinking through a problem or forming his opinion, but actually, said Stevenson, he's probably responding to a linguistic design of some sort — to the covert, insidious "influence of jingling words." In "The Coast of Fife," Stevenson shared an anecdote from one of his former Edinburgh teachers who, as a boy, had formed a Philosophical Society with some schoolfellows.

Before these learned pundits, one member laid the following ingenious problem: 'What would be the result of putting a pound of potassium in a pot of porter?' 'I should think there would be a number of interesting bi-products,' said a smatterer at my elbow; but for me

the tale itself has a bi-product, and stands as a type
of much that is most human. For this inquirer who
conceived himself to burn with a zeal entirely chemical,
was really immersed in a design of a quite different
nature; unconsciously to his own recently breeched
intelligence, he was engaged in literature. Putting,
pound, potassium, pot, porter; initial *p*, mediant *t*—
that was his idea, poor little boy!

All manipulators of people's minds, from time immemorial,
have exploited this instinctive attention to rhythm, sound,
and patterns of language. "So with politics and that which
excites men in the present," wrote Stevenson, "so with history and that which rouses them in the past: there lie at the
root of what appears most serious unsuspected elements."[24]
In his essay "Beggars," Stevenson drew a curious lesson
about the persistence of the literary in people's lives. There
was an unpensioned "old soldier" he met with occasionally
on his walks in the country around Edinburgh. Destitute
and barely literate, with "his toes looking out of his boots,
and his shirt looking out of his elbows, and death looking out of his smile, and his big, crazy frame shaken by ac-
cesses of cough," this old soldier possessed very definite literary tastes. "Keats—John Keats, sir—and Shelley were his
favourite bards," Stevenson recalled. "What took him was a
richness in the speech; he loved the exotic, the unexpected
word; the moving cadence of a phrase; a vague sense of emotion (about nothing) in the very letters of the alphabet: the
romance of language." Another tramp, a knife-grinder, "a
little, lean, and fiery man, with the eyes of a dog and the
face of a gipsy," was just the opposite. He had a "vulgar taste
in letters; scarce flying higher than the story papers." Yet
Stevenson gave him his due. "But if he had no fine sense of
poetry in letters, he felt with a deep joy the poetry of life.
You should have heard him speak of what he loved; of the
tent pitched beside the talking water; of the stars overhead

at night; of the blest return of morning, the peep of day over the moors, the awaking birds among the birches." The first tramp, "lover of the literary bards," had been in the Indian Mutiny; he had fought with famous men, witnessed scenes of horror and valor. Yet when Stevenson asked him about these experiences, he had no more to say than "hot work, sir!" "His life was naught to him, the vivid pages of experience quite blank," Stevenson mused. "[I]n words his pleasure lay—melodious, agitated words—printed words, about that which he had never seen and was connatally incapable of comprehending."[25]

These two mendicants were unsophisticated, hard-scrabble people, entirely untrained in literary art. Yet for RLS, their characters were boldly outlined in relation to literature. The old soldier, he thought, was "the artist, the lover and artificer of words." The knife-grinder was "the maker, the seeër, [sic] the lover and forger of experience." Yet if the children of these two beggars had met and married, Stevenson wondered, might not "some illustrious writer count descent from the beggar-soldier and the needy knife-grinder?"[26]

A writer should try to bring into unity the love of language and the love of life. Nor should he seek to place one over the other. He can, and should, practice his technique. But no trick of style can be extracted from the texture of experience. "And thus I lived with words," Stevenson said of his literary apprenticeship. Not to adventure ebulliently among words defeats the whole purpose of writing. Why play it safe? And there are moral stakes here, as well. For predictable, run-of-the-mill discourse dulls our perceptions by its repetitiveness. Style *wakes us up*. And for insight and knowledge to get through to the reader at all, "[o]ur attention requires to be surprised."[27]

Style is not a knack a writer acquires and then programs into his work, like software. Style is organic. It springs from the writer's intentions and his desires for his art. While his contemporaries were grinding prose "with regularity and with a certain commercial fineness," wrote James, Stevenson kept his individuality. His only rule was curiosity, and so each of his books represents an independent effort—"a window opened to a different view."[28] If a style doesn't change and evolve, it's not breathing anymore, and the writer has thrown in the towel. If there was any secret to Stevenson's style, it was his versatility and his willingness to experiment. Thus all great artists, he said, from Raphael to Shakespeare to Beethoven, adopted a style to match the force of their vision in any new undertaking. "Every fresh work in which they embark is the signal for a fresh engagement of the whole forces of their mind; and the changing views which accompany the growth of their experience are marked by still more sweeping alterations in the manner of their art."[29]

DREAMS

. . . .

THE LAND OF NOD

From breakfast on through all the day
At home among my friends I stay,
But every night I go abroad
Afar into the land of Nod.

All by myself I have to go,
With none to tell me what to do —
All alone beside the streams
And up the mountain-sides of dreams.

The strangest things are there for me,
Both things to eat and things to see,
And many frightening sights abroad
Till morning in the Land of Nod.

Try as I like to find the way,
I never can get back by day,
Nor can remember plain and clear
The curious music that I hear.[1]

When Stevenson was a child, bedtime was the preserve of
fantasies, picture-making, and stories—the curious music
of the subconscious. Stevenson claimed that his mind was
most active in the hours between being put to bed and falling asleep: "I remember these periods more distinctly and I
believe further back than any other part of my childhood."[2]
Some of the images summoned in those nighttime vigils
stayed with him all his life.

Many poems in *A Child's Garden of Verses* are about

going to bed and waking up, the transitional world between daylight and nighttime. The child in these poems, literally and mentally, floats between two symbolic planes of existence. The poem called "Night and Day" begins,

> When the golden day is done,
> > Through the closing portal,
> Child and garden, flower and sun,
> > Vanish all things mortal.
>
> As the blinding shadows fall
> > As the rays diminish,
> Under evening's cloak they all
> > Roll away and vanish.[3]

The garden, the flower, the sun, *and the child* disappear into dark shadows. When night falls, everything retreats inward, creeps inside itself. Some poems hint at a deviant desire for this nightworld. In "Escape at Bedtime," the child slips outside to gaze up at the night sky and the constellations that glitter and wink at him in the dark. In "My Bed Is a Boat" he is off on a solitary journey into the unknown.

> My bed is like a little boat;
> > Nurse helps me in when I embark;
> She girds me in my sailor's coat
> > And starts me in the dark.
>
> At night I go on board and say
> > Good-night to all my friends on shore;
> I shut my eyes and sail away
> > And see and hear no more.
>
> All night across the dark we steer:
> > But when the day returns at last,
> Safe in my room, beside the pier,
> > I find my vessel fast.[4]

In the poem "Young Night Thought," the child anticipates the pleasure of going to bed because that's when his imagination starts working.

> All night long and every night,
> When my mamma puts out the light,
> I see the people marching by,
> As plain as day, before my eye.
>
> Armies and emperors and kings,
> All carrying different kinds of things,
> And marching in so grand a way,
> You never saw the like by day.
> . . . .
> At first they move a little slow,
> But still the faster on they go,
> And still beside them close I keep
> Until we reach the town of Sleep.[5]

There is also in these poems a curious wish to be small or to hide. He envies the toy soldier who is buried in a hole:

> He has lived, a little thing,
> In the grassy woods of spring;
> Done, if he could tell me true,
> Just as I should like to do.[6]

In "My Kingdom," the child escapes to a "very little dell / No higher than my head" where he rules over the "little pool," "the little hills," "the little sparrows, "the little minnows."

> Alas! and as my home I neared,
> How very big my nurse appeared,
>   How great and cool the rooms![7]

He imagines being at the bottom of a river:

> Sailing blossoms, silver fishes,
>   Paven pools as clear as air—

How a child wishes
To live down there![8]

Another world could be summoned just by closing his eyes to the everyday and entering a private refuge from boredom.

When at home alone I sit
And am very tired of it,
I have just to shut my eyes
To go sailing through the skies—
To go sailing far away
To the pleasant Land of Play;
To the fairy land afar
Where the Little People are[.]

And in his mind the child really goes there, becomes "a tiny self" climbing blades of grass, sailing on a leaf in a puddle, until he returns with open eyes into the alien world of grown-ups and their incomprehensible realities.

When my eyes I once again
Open, and see all things plain:
High bare walls, great bare floor;
Great big knobs on drawer and door;
Great big people perched on chairs,
Stitching tucks and mending tears,
Each a hill that I could climb,
And talking nonsense all the time—
      O dear me,
      That I could be
A sailor on the rain-pool sea,
A climber in the clover tree,
And just come back, a sleepy-head,
Late at night to go to bed.[9]

To go to bed—where dreams and the imagination are in command, and anything can happen.

When the lamps were taken away at bedtime, Stevenson remembered, "I told myself romances in which I played the hero. Now and then the subject would be the animation of my playthings; but usually these fantasies embraced the adventures of a lifetime, full of far journeys and Homeric battles." Built to the pitch of epics, he always ended the adventure gloriously: "I never left myself till I was dead."[10] In this way, little Louis could slip away into kingdoms of his own creation. He was all at once author, actor, and audience of his own drama. It seemed like a trick, flying from this world to another and back again at will. Space and time were unfixed and mutable, measured in a syllable or in a second.

The grammar of dreams is strikingly similar to that of the literary imagination. As Stevenson observed to Owen Wister, "dreams are merely novels, they are made with every sort of literary trick; a word stands for a year, if it is the right word, equally with the reader and the dreamer."[11] For both, it's just a matter of believing in the illusion as if it were really happening. It *is* really happening. When he was asked whether he believed dreams came true, Stevenson reportedly said, "Certainly, they are just as real as anything else."[12]

Some of the poems in *A Child's Garden of Verses* make the nighttime world seem enchanted and benign. It was not. "My childhood was in reality a very mixed experience, full of fever, nightmare, insomnia, painful days and interminable nights," Stevenson wrote to William Archer, "and I can speak with less authority of Gardens than of that other 'land of counterpane.'"[13] In "A Good Boy," the child is eager to get to bed—"My bed is waiting cool and fresh, with linen smooth and fair"—but there's a little desperation attached to his pleasure:

> I know that, till to-morrow I shall see the sun arise,
> No ugly dream shall fright my mind, no ugly sight my
>   eyes,

But slumber hold me tightly till I waken in the dawn,
And hear the thrushes singing in the lilacs round the
    lawn.[14]

Going to bed at night is something he both seeks, to hold
him tight against reality, and an ordeal he has to get through.
The three poems in "North-West Passage" evoke a harrowing trek in the "haunted night" to the "long black passage up
to bed." The second poem is called "Shadow March."

All round the house is the jet-black night;
    It stares through the window-pane;
It crawls in the corners, hiding from the light,
    And it moves with the moving flame.

Now my little heart goes a-beating like a drum,
    With the breath of the Bogie in my hair;
And all round the candle the crooked shadows come
    And go marching along up the stair.

The shadow of the balusters, the shadow of the lamp,
    The shadow of the child that goes to bed—
All the wicked shadows coming, tramp, tramp, tramp,
    With the black night overhead.[15]

In the poem "My Shadow" the child's shadow is, again, both
the happy child, himself, and a mischievous, dark projection, a second self—the reverse image to the magic of the
street-lamps and the beams of the Stevenson lighthouses.
Shady counterparts to the good little boy.

. . . . . .

Stevenson was a systematic and dutiful laborer, and he
couldn't comprehend how anyone could write without a
regimen. He wrote to Walter Simpson, "I wonder what you
do without regular habits of work. I am capable of only
two theories of existence: the industrious worker's, the
spreester's; all between seems blank to me."[16] Although he

. . . . . .

kept himself well in hand, Stevenson was always deeply intrigued by the mystery of the creative impulses. The poem "The Wind" feels like an invocation or playful impersonation of the Romantic lyric voice. How can it not be?

> I saw the different things you did,
> But always you yourself you hid.
> I felt you push, I heard you call,
> I could not see yourself at all—
>> O wind, a-blowing all day long,
>> O wind, that sings so loud a song!
>
> O you that are so strong and cold,
> O blower, are you young or old?
> Are you a beast of field and tree,
> Or just a stronger child than me?
>> O wind, a-blowing all day long,
>> O wind, that sings so loud a song![17]

In Shelley's famous "Ode to the West Wind," the poet wishes to be overwhelmed by the Muse. Stevenson joked, "I once called myself (not without applause) Shelley and water"; and in "The Wind," there's the faintest echo of "Make me thy lyre!"[18] There are multiple selves in writers, stronger, more aggressive selves: "I felt you push, I heard you call." Often enough Stevenson wasn't sure where his tales were coming from—were they something in his past, in memories, or in other, less accessible recesses of his nature? Who is the wind? Who are the unseen playmates, the speechless playthings, the Little People, the foreign children, the fairies who name the flowers? Who is "The Dumb Soldier," buried in a hole in the springtime, that needs the child to make up a story about what he saw there?

> When the grass was closely mown,
> Walking on the lawn alone,
> In the turf a hole I found
> And hid a soldier underground.

Spring and daisies came apace;
Grasses hide my hiding place;
Grasses run like a green sea
O'er the lawn up to my knee.

Under grass alone he lies,
Looking up with leaden eyes,
Scarlet coat and pointed gun,
To the stars and to the sun.

When the grass is ripe like grain,
When the scythe is stoned again,
When the lawn is shaven clear,
Then my hole shall reappear.

I shall find him, never fear,
I shall find my grenadier;
But for all that's gone and come,
I shall find my soldier dumb.

He has lived, a little thing,
In the grassy woods of spring;
Done, if I could tell me true,
Just as I should like to do.

He has seen the starry hours
And the springing of the flowers;
And the fairy things that pass
In the forests of the grass.

In the silence he has heard
Talking bee and ladybird,
And the butterfly has flown
O'er him as he lay alone.

Not a word will he disclose,
Not a word of all he knows.
I must lay him on the shelf,
And make up the tale myself.[19]

It's like a journey into the underworld, a myth of death and rebirth in which the self discovers a voice within, or absorbs the mystic voices of others who work through him: "In the silence he has heard / Talking bee and ladybird."

In these surprising poems, many of them written when Stevenson was severely ill, the child, like Orpheus, who descends alone into the dark, into the dream or the make-believe world, is an analog for the artist's journey into the subterraneous parts of the self and the imagination — a psychic vagabonding. Stevenson's child is also chameleon-like in his capacity to imagine himself in many roles. He plays, he invents. He transcends the outside world and reality. If it is raining, he stays at home and makes a city of his blocks. If the adults are busy, he disappears into the land of picture-storybooks. He is observant of phenomena, even hyper-observant. But he is essentially solitary and inward. The "little book which is all about my childhood," as Stevenson quaintly called it in a letter to Cummy, can feel like a probing of the sources of personality or a veiled confession of existential loneliness.[20] "And the butterfly has flown / O'er him as he lay alone," he sings, conjuring an image of a lost soul. "All by myself I have to go," says the child departing for the Land of Nod. "All night across the dark we steer," he prays, clinging to his boat. This is the human imagination as survival.

· · · · · ·

Half of Stevenson's childhood seems to have been spent in the grip of the night-hag, who "would have him by the throat, and pluck him strangling and screaming, from his sleep."[21] From early childhood until he was about thirteen, Stevenson claimed he was "an ardent and uncomfortable dreamer."[22] He recalled nightmares brought on by fever in which "the room swelled and shrank, and his clothes, hanging on a nail, now loomed up instant to the bigness of a church, and now drew away into a horror of infinite distance and

· · · · · ·

infinite littleness."[23] "I had an extreme terror of Hell, implanted in me, I suppose, by my good nurse," Stevenson confessed, "which used to haunt me terribly on stormy nights, when the wind had broken loose and was going about the town like a bedlamite."[24] He always hated the sound of the wind during a storm, even in Samoa, and he wrote at least two memorable poems about being haunted by the sound of the wind.[25] It was like a "durable and unvarying ... heathen deity," he said, or a cloaked horseman riding eternally to the bottom of the street and back again, all night long.[26] "I think even now that I hear the terrible *howl* of his passage. ... On such nights I would lie awake and pray and cry, until I prayed and cried myself to sleep."[27]

Stevenson credited Cummy with stirring in him a strong sense for the dramatic (he dedicated *A Child's Garden of Verses* to her). When he was delirious with fever, he had a series of dreams, "for a good many years," his mother claimed, about a mysterious "Mrs. Sauley." With tears running down his cheeks, he would cry out desperately, "O, send the parcel to Mrs. Sauley!"[28] He remembered a terrifying dream about a peculiar, loathsome shade of brown, like sealskin, and another in which he had to swallow the world. In her diary for February 6, 1855, his mother recorded, "Lou dreamed that 'he heard the noise of pens writing.'"[29] A branch scraping the windowpane? A guttering lamp? An eerie, premonitory sound for a boy with Lou's propensities.

· · · · · ·

Dreamers are like writers, and also like readers, and like children—people who don't particularly want to distinguish between real and fictional events. Dreams and memories, make-believe and reality are intermingled. One part of the self watches the antics of the other. The inner or nocturnal world feels more intense than the day-lit rational world we work and talk and make decisions in. Who can draw the line between them? "There is no distinction on the face of our experiences," Stevenson wrote, "one is vivid indeed, and one dull, and one pleasant, and another agonising to remember; but which of them is what we call true, and which a dream, there is not one hair to prove." We may remain just as active asleep as when we are awake, for what is the difference between "the treasures of memory that all men review for their amusement" and "the harvests of their dreams"?[30]

If we take him at his word, Stevenson was a practiced harvester of dreams, which he "turned to account" in the trade of storytelling. "I am quite in the habit of dreaming stories," he told an American interviewer. "The fact is that I am so much in the habit of making stories that I go on making them while I sleep quite as hard, apparently, as when I am awake. They sometimes come to me in the form of nightmares, in so far that they make me cry out aloud." Even when he was fast asleep, he said he knew he was inventing: "when I cry out it is with gratification to know that the story is so good. So soon as I awake, and it always awakens me when I get on a good thing, I set to work and put it together."[31] In his famous essay "A Chapter on Dreams," written when he was living at Saranac Lake, Stevenson described the "Brownies" who pulled the strings of his imagination, the "Little People" responsible for the genesis of *Strange Case of Dr. Jekyll and Mr. Hyde*, "Olalla," and other tales. It took some concentration to harness this inner resource. When he was an amateur dreamer, he claimed, he dreamed stories for pleasure, irresponsible little tales, "where a thread might be dropped, or one adventure quitted for another, on fancy's least suggestion. So that the little people who manage man's internal theatre had not as yet received a very rigorous training; and played upon their stage like children who should have slipped into the house and found it empty, rather than like drilled actors performing a set piece to a huge hall of faces."[32] When he became a professional author, though, he had to become a more disciplined dreamer. Especially when the butcher was at the back gate, his little people had to bestir themselves with energy.

Jekyll and Hyde seemed to have come to him when he was in a relaxed mental state. "For two days I went about racking my brains for a plot of any sort," Stevenson wrote. But the story came to him when he stopped racking. He dreamed some of the key scenes, and that was enough to get it going. "All the rest was made awake, and consciously, although I think I can trace in much of it the manner of my Brownies."[33] Stevenson makes it sound like a magic trick. In Fanny's account, though, the gestation and composition of the tale was informed by his anger at her criticism—she wanted it to be more than a shilling shocker—and his intense loyalty to the dream origins of the tale. "Louis wrote Jekyll and Hyde with great rapidity on the lines of his dream. In the small hours of one morning I was wakened by cries of horror from him. I, thinking he had a nightmare, waked him. He said, angrily, 'Why did you wake me? I was dreaming a fine boguey tale.' I had waked him at the first transformation scene. He had had in his mind an idea of a double life story, but it was not the same as the dream." Fanny advised Stevenson that his obsession with the dream hampered the story, that "here was a great moral allegory that the dream was obscuring."[34] Stevenson, boiling over this criticism, threw the pages into the fire and immediately began to write another story. He finished it in about six weeks. As he wrote to F. W. H. Meyers, the book was "conceived, written, re-written, re-re-written, and printed inside ten weeks."[35] In Lloyd Osbourne's more exciting version of these events, the book was written in fewer than six days in a frenzy of composition by an author completely and demoniacally possessed by his muse. Thus, apocryphally, a classic was given to the world.

That a novel about good and evil, crime, transgression, and our divided nature had its source in an author's dark subconscious has contributed to the popularity and the mystique of *Jekyll and Hyde*. But Stevenson claimed that he "had long been trying to write a story on this subject, to find a body, a vehicle, for that strong sense of a man's double being which must at times come in upon and overwhelm the mind of every thinking creature."[36] In letters he exchanged with Meyers, a psychologist and one of the founders of the London Psychical Society, Stevenson described in detail (listed as cases A, B, C, D) his own experience of harboring within himself two separate people. It is a fascinating letter and clear evidence that Stevenson was accustomed to tracking his mental states. Sometimes he could even disentangle the "two consciousnesses." He called them *myself* and *the other fellow*. He wrote that the dreamer in "A Chapter on Dreams" was probably this *other fellow*, the part of himself that could be mischievous or helpful, sprightly or tame, but was more or less out of his conscious control.[37]

There is something uncanny about the process of literary composition, the enigma of authorship. Like many writers, Stevenson was sharply tuned to his mental life. Though a disciplined and systematic writer, he welcomed the possibility that his stories originated within a part of his personality he didn't understand—the Brownies, the little people, the shadow self, the other fellow. A writer may create out of a subconscious need to locate certain energies within himself, parts of the psyche he thought he had evicted but that still want his attention. In the early twentieth century, Carl Jung would claim that there are sinister, shadowy selves that demand to be recognized, and some dream theories holds that all the characters in our dreams are facets of ourselves. This is the crucial psychological insight expressed in *Jekyll and Hyde*. Keenly aware of his own sense of duality, Stevenson astutely perceived that Henry Jekyll's first acquaintance with his other self, the troglodytic, dwarfish, ape-like Hyde, would not be one of revulsion but rather of appalled recognition. "And yet when I looked upon that ugly idol in the glass, I was conscious of no repugnance, rather of a leap of welcome. *This, too, was myself*."[38]

It seems highly unlikely that Sigmund Freud, whose *Interpretation of Dreams* was published five years after Stevenson's death, ever read "A Chapter on Dreams." Yet Stevenson posits no less than the Freudian claim that only a filament separates our conscious and unconscious lives—if even a filament. Stevenson didn't need the new science of psychoanalysis to explain to him that dreams, memories, and art are interrelated, maybe interdependent. Creative work takes place in an intermediate space between cognition and intuition. Stevenson made himself take notice when stories, scenes, or people chanced to drift in and pay a visit, in sleep, in daydreams, or in a creative trance. Who knows what drives the pen to scratch? And writing often feels like trying to describe a dream to someone. The dream is so substantive, so real, but at the same time so impossible to grasp, like trapping fog in a net. To try to recount it in everyday prose seems thin and inadequate. Stevenson very often said that what he wrote was a poor substitute for how he felt. It was all too deep to get at with language. Life is so ephemeral, transient, ever vanishing—*incommunicable* was his word.

· · · · · ·

Dr. Jekyll and Mr. Hyde has always been to me a very dreamlike book—a yellowish-umber, underwater dream. The layers of brown fog hanging over the town (Edinburgh, surely, as G. K. Chesterton noted, not London), the "foggy cupola" of the surgical theater, the "watery green" potion. The writing is roily and pungent—to Vladimir Nabokov, the book had "a delightful winey taste."[39] No film can do justice to the evocativeness of Stevenson's prose, and in speeding along to discover the heart of the mystery, we can fail to notice the mastery of the author's choice of words, their sounds, the pace of the phrasing, all of it contributing to an atmosphere of inescapable strangeness, of closing in. "The fog still slept on the wing above the drowned city, where the lamps glimmered like carbuncles; and through the muffle and smother of these fallen clouds, the procession of the town's life was still rolling in through the great arteries with a sound as of a mighty wind."[40] After the brutal murder of Sir Danvers Carew, the lawyer Mr. Utterson, sick at heart, takes a police inspector to Hyde's house in Soho.

It was by this time about nine in the morning, and the first fog of the season. A great chocolate-coloured pall lowered over heaven, but the wind was continually charging and routing these embattled vapours; so that as the cab crawled from street to street, Mr. Utterson beheld a marvellous number of degrees and hues of twilight; for here it would be dark like the back-end of evening; and there would be a glow of a rich, lurid brown, like the light of some strange conflagration; and here, for a moment, the fog would be quite broken up, and a haggard shaft of daylight would glance in between the swirling wreaths. The dismal quarter of Soho seen under these changing glimpses, with its muddy ways, and slatternly passengers, and its lamps, which had never been extinguished or had been kindled afresh to combat this mournful re-invasion of darkness, seemed, in the lawyer's eyes, like a district of some city in a nightmare.[41]

The drowned city, the carbuncular lamps and slatternly people, the chocolate pall, the lurid chiaroscuro of the metropolis hovering between darkness and light. The imagery invokes Baudelaire and Dante, forecasts T. S. Eliot's modern wasteland. The suspense and density of the mood feel like a prickling of the skin. The reader shares with Mr. Utterson a vague, menacing knowledge that can't be named, like being startled, for a split second, by a glimpse of an unfamiliar face in the mirror. Truly, like something dreamed.

The dream that made Stevenson cry out in his sleep—the dream that gave him the transformation scene—probably happened in September 1885. A little more than ten years before, at age twenty-five, he was studying for the bar at Edinburgh University and living with his parents at 17 Heriot Row. He had already decided he didn't want to pursue engineering or law, that he wanted to become a writer. A couple of his essays had been published in magazines. He had also written his *Fables*, haunting little parables that remained unpublished for twenty years. But he was frustrated and knew he could wring more from himself.

Two months before taking the bar exam, Stevenson rattled off to Colvin an idea for a tale. "The story is to be called 'When the Devil was Well': scene, Italy, Renaissance; colour purely imaginary of course, my own unregenerate idea of what Italy then was: the frame somewhat good, but perhaps a little involved, perhaps not quite enough *d'un seul jet*."[42] Stevenson finished "When the Devil Was Well" the next year; but the "unfavorable opinion of his friends was accepted as final," according to Graham Balfour, and the story was not published until the Boston Bibliophile Society discovered the manuscript, in 1921.[43]

Maybe that's for the best. Stevenson was full of stories in those years, full of the dream of writing. The imagination incubates, sometimes for a long time. In 1875, Stevenson was grasping at the kinds of tales he wanted to write—what he was waiting to write. In the same letter to Colvin, he seems to burst out with an utterance that, it turns out, was both wish and prophecy. "O when shall I find the story of my dreams, that shall never halt nor wander nor step aside, but go ever before its face and ever swifter and louder, until the pit receives it, roaring?"[44]

ACKNOWLEDGMENTS

At the University of Iowa Press, Elisabeth Chretien and Catherine Cocks guided this book with never failing cheerfulness and professionalism. The Muse Books series is under the general editorship of distinguished biographer Robert Richardson. I feel privileged to be a part of the series, and I'm grateful to Professor Richardson for his support for this project.

Some material was published as "Stevenson's Mortal Questions" in *Victorians Institute Journal* 42 (2014). Thanks to the editors for permission to reprint.

Thanks are also due to the Edna T. Shaeffer Humanist Award committee in the College of Arts and Letters at James Madison University and to dean David K. Jeffrey.

On a gray afternoon in November 2015, I idly Googled the words "Booth and Mehew." The very first hit was a British vendor on eBay who had a set of the *Collected Letters* at auction for £65.00—a steal. To own all eight volumes of Stevenson's radiant letters while writing this book was like a gift from the universe. Thank you, eBay seller, whoever you are.

John Macfie, the current resident of 17 Heriot Row, answered my inquiries about his street lamp and supplied facts about the history of Edinburgh's street lamps that I was able to use in chapter 1. I am grateful for his generous correspondence.

Immeasurable love and gratitude to Chuck Dotas. Your life-lovingness buoys me up. Your love lights my way. "Mine eyes were swift to know thee, and my heart / As swift to love."

Stevenson's letters reveal again and again how much he valued the friends in his life. "But we are all travellers in what John Bunyan calls the wilderness of this world," he wrote, "and the best that we can find in our travels is an honest friend." I am grateful to Laurie Lakebrink, honest friend for more than three decades, headstrong believer in the romance of life.

A NOTE ON SOURCES

The New Edinburgh Edition of the *Collected Works of Robert Louis Stevenson* is in process under the general editorship of Stephen Arata, Richard Dury, Penny Fielding, and Anthony Mandal. This groundbreaking edition will finally offer scholars accurate versions of all of Stevenson's works, with careful annotations and comprehensive introductory materials.

The whole of Stevenson's essays are not, to my knowledge, available in one convenient, affordable edition. Robert-Louis-Stevenson.org is a valuable resource for locating Stevenson's works. The essay collections he compiled himself include *Virginibus Puerisque* (1881), *Familiar Studies of Men and Books* (1882), *Memories and Portraits* (1887), and *Across the Plains* (1892). Most of his other essays, originally published in magazines, have been collected under various organizational principles. A few reliable paperback editions are *The Lantern-Bearers and Other Essays*, chosen by Jeremy Treglown (1988), Claire Harman's *R. L. Stevenson: Essays and Poems* (1992), and *R. L. Stevenson on Fiction: An Anthology of Literary and Critical Essays*, edited by Glenda Norquay (1999). *The Complete Stories of Robert Louis Stevenson*, edited by Barry Menikoff (2002) gives you *Jekyll and Hyde* and nineteen other tales, including *The Suicide Club, The Rajah's Diamond*, and *The Merry Men*. Roslyn Jolly has edited Stevenson's *South Sea Tales* for Oxford World's Classics (2008). *Travels with a Donkey in the Cévennes* and *The Amateur Emigrant* are available in one paperback, edited by Christopher MacLachlan (2005). There are dozens of editions, many illustrated, of *A Child's Garden of Verses*. My source for Stevenson's poetry is the second edition of Janet Adam Smith's *Collected Poems* (1971).

Biographies that have received critical praise are *Voyage to Windward* by J. C. Furnas (1951), *Robert Louis Stevenson* by James Pope-Hennessy (1974), and *Dreams of Exile* by Ian Bell (1992). I have chiefly consulted Claire Harman's *Myself and the Other Fel-*

low (2005), as well as Graham Balfour's two-volume *The Life of Robert Louis Stevenson* (1901).

Bradford A. Booth and Ernest Mehew's eight-volume *The Letters of Robert Louis Stevenson* (Yale University Press, 1995) has been indispensable. All letters are from this edition. *Robert Louis Stevenson: Interviews and Recollections*, edited by Reginald Charles Terry (University of Iowa Press, 1996), is a collection of excerpts from published memoirs of Stevenson. It's diverting and illuminating reading for Stevensonians, as is John Alexander Hammerton's *Stevensoniana* (Grant Richards, 1903). Paul Maixner's *Robert Louis Stevenson: The Critical Heritage* (Routledge & Kegan Paul, 1981) is a substantive source for understanding how Stevenson was read and reviewed by his contemporaries.

NOTES

· · · · · · · · · · · · · · · · ·

PREFACE

1   S. S. McClure in *Robert Louis Stevenson: Interviews and Recollections*, ed. R. C. Terry (Iowa City: University of Iowa Press, 1996), 124.

2   Robert Louis Stevenson, *Travels with a Donkey in the Cévennes* (New York: Penguin, 2004), 32.

3   Stevenson, "On Some Technical Elements of Style in Literature," in *Essays of Travel and in the Art of Writing* (New York: Scribner's, 1905), 253–54. https://archive.org /stream/essaysoftravelinoostev#page/n5/mode/2up.

4   Ibid.

RLS

1   "New Export of Old Lanterns," *Glasgow Herald*, April 19, 1960.

2   Stevenson, "The Lamplighter," in *Robert Louis Stevenson: Collected Poems*, ed. Janet Adam Smith (New York: Viking, 1971), 380.

3   Stevenson, "A Plea for Gas Lamps," in *Virginibus Puerisque and Other Papers* (London: C. Kegan Paul, 1881), 292–93. http://www.archive.org/stream/buspuerisstevvirginirich #page/n5/mode/2up.

4   Stevenson, *Edinburgh: Picturesque Notes* (London: Pallas, 2001), 44, 16; "The Foreigner at Home," in *R. L. Stevenson: Essays and Poems*, ed. Claire Harman (London: Everyman, 1992), 19; "'A Penny Plain and Twopence Coloured,'" in Harman, *Essays and Poems*, 64.

5   Stevenson, "My First Book: *Treasure Island*," in Harman, *Essays and Poems*, 209.

6   G. K. Chesterton, *Varied Types* (New York: Dodd, Mead, 1901), 101.

7 Stevenson, "The Lantern-Bearers," in *The Lantern-Bearers and Other Essays*, ed. Jeremy Treglown (New York: Farrar, Straus & Giroux, 1988), 232.

8 Robert Louis Stevenson to Sidney Colvin, September 30, 1892, in *The Letters of Robert Louis Stevenson*, ed. Bradford A. Booth and Ernest Mayhew (New Haven: Yale University Press, 1995), 7:384. All subsequent citations of letters by RLS are from the specified volume of Booth and Mayhew, unless otherwise stated.

9 Henry James, quoted in Terry, *Interviews and Recollections*, 61n1.

10 Sidney Colvin, in Terry, *Interviews and Recollections*, 65.

11 Stevenson, "Diogenes," in *The Works of Robert Louis Stevenson*, Vailima Edition (New York: Charles Scribner's Sons, 1923), 26:17.

12 Stevenson, "The Lantern-Bearers," in Treglown, *The Lantern-Bearers*, 232.

13 Stevenson to Katharine de Mattos, October 1874, 2:63.

14 Stevenson to Angela Plomer, August 18, 1893, 8:154.

15 Stevenson to Will H. Low, March 1883, 4:87.

16 Stevenson, "A College Magazine," in *Memories and Portraits* (New York: Scribner's, 1895), 57–58. http://www.archive.org /stream/memoriesandportroostev#page/n13/mode/2up.

17 Ibid., 59.

18 Ibid.

19 Stevenson to A. Trevor Haddon, July 5, 1883, 4:141.

20 Stevenson, "A College Magazine," in *Memories and Portraits*, 61.

21 Stevenson, "The Education of an Engineer," in Treglown, *The Lantern-Bearers*, 251.

22 Stevenson, "A College Magazine," in *Memories and Portraits*, 61.

23 Stevenson to Bob Stevenson, November 17, 1868, 1:168.

24 Stevenson to Frances Sitwell, November 17, 1873, 1:372.

25 Stevenson to Frances Sitwell, February 5, 1875, 2:114.

26 Stevenson to Bob Stevenson, November 17, 1868, 1:168.

27 Stevenson, "A Note on Realism," in *Essays of Travel and in the Art of Writing*, 278.

28 Stevenson to Katharine de Mattos, October 1874, 2:62.

29 Stevenson to Charles Robertson, late 1878 or early 1879, 2:295–96.

30 Adelaide Boodle, in Terry, *Interviews and Recollections*, 103–4.

31 Stevenson to Sidney Colvin, March 9, 1884, 4:246.

32 Stevenson, "My First Book," in Harman, *Essays and Poems*, 209.

33 Stevenson to George Iles, October 29, 1887, 6:47.

34 Stevenson, "Fontainebleau," in *Across the Plains* (London: Chatto & Windus, 1892), 114. https://archive.org/stream /withoostevacrossplainsrich#page/n5/mode/2up.

35 Stevenson, "A Gossip on Romance," in *The Lantern-Bearers*, 175.

36 Henry James, *Partial Portraits* (Westport, CT: Greenwood, 1970), 156.

37 Stevenson to Edmund Gosse, January 2, 1886, 5:172.

38 Stevenson to John Addington Symonds, early March 1886, 5:221.

39 Stevenson to George Meredith, September 5, 1893, 8:163–64.

40 Stevenson, dedication to *Catriona*, in *"Kidnapped" and "Catriona"* (Oxford: Oxford University Press, 1986), 211.

41 Stevenson, *The Silverado Squatters* (London: Chatto & Windus, 1910), 35. https://archive.org/stream/silverado squasteoostev#page/n9/mode/2up.

42 Stevenson to Sidney Colvin, April 2, 1889, 6:276.

43 Stevenson to Henry James, August 19, 1890, 6:403.

44 Stevenson to Sidney Colvin, May 21, 1893, 8:70.

45 Isobel Field, in Terry, *Interviews and Recollections*, 190.

46 Stevenson to Sidney Colvin, May 25, 1892, 7:287.

47 Fanny Stevenson to Anne Jenkin, December 5, 1894, 8:409.

48 Sidney Colvin to Robert Louis Stevenson, March 21, 1894, 8:279n.

49 Edward Burne-Jones to Sidney Colvin, in *Robert Louis*

Stevenson: The Critical Heritage, ed. Paul Maixner (London: Routledge & Kegan Paul, 1981), 440.

50 Stevenson, *The Silverado Squatters*, 35.

51 Stevenson to Frances Sitwell, October 9, 1873, 1:336.

52 Stevenson to Henry James, May 28, 1888, 6:197.

53 Ibid.

54 Stevenson to Sidney Colvin, June 6, 1893, 8:91.

55 Margaret Stevenson, "Notes about Robert Louis Stevenson from his Mother's Diary," in *The Works of Robert Louis Stevenson*, 26:310.

56 Walter Benjamin, "The Storyteller," in *Illuminations*, trans. Harry Zohn (New York: Schocken Books, 1969), 83, 108–9.

57 Stevenson, dedication to *Catriona*, in *"Kidnapped" and "Catriona,"* 211.

58 Stevenson to Sidney Colvin, June 6, 1893, 8:91.

ROMANCE

1 Stevenson to John Meiklejohn, February 1, 1880, 3:61–62.

2 Stevenson to A. Trevor Haddon, April 23 or 24, 1884, 4:275–76.

3 Stevenson to W. E. Henley, June 1884, 4:307.

4 Stevenson, "A Penny Plain and Twopence Coloured," in Harman, *Essays and Poems*, 67–68.

5 G. K. Chesterton, *Robert Louis Stevenson* (New York: Hodder and Stoughton, 1927), 51–52.

6 Stevenson, "'A Penny Plain and Twopence Coloured,'" in Harman, *Essays and Poems*, 67.

7 Stevenson to W. E. Henley, November 23, 1883, 4:207.

8 Stevenson, "'A Penny Plain and Twopence Coloured,'" in Harman, *Essays and Poems*, 66.

9 Stevenson, "A Gossip on Romance," in Treglown, *The Lantern-Bearers*, 172, 174, 172.

10 Stevenson, "Walt Whitman," in Harman, *Essays and Poems*, 135.

11 Stevenson, *Kidnapped* (Oxford: Oxford University Press, 2014), 122.

12 Hilary Mantel, interview by Mona Simpson, "Art of Fiction No. 226," *Paris Review* 212 (Spring 2015). https://www .theparisreview.org/interviews/6360/hilary-mantel-art-of -fiction-no-226-hilary-mantel.

13 Stevenson, dedication to *Kidnapped*, 3.

14 Stevenson, "A Gossip on a Novel of Dumas's," in *Memories and Portraits*, 244.

15 Theodore Watts-Dunton, in Maixner, *Critical Heritage*, 242.

16 Stevenson to Theodore Watts-Dunton, early September 1886, 5:313.

17 Stevenson, "Some Gentlemen in Fiction," *Scribner's Magazine* (June 1888), 764. http://ebooks.library.cornell.edu/cgi/t /text/pageviewer-idx?c=scri;cc=scri;rgn=full%20text;idno =scrio003-6;didno=scrio003-6;view=image;seq=0772;node =scrio003-6%3A14.

18 Fanny Stevenson, in Terry, *Interviews and Recollections*, 185–86.

19 Isobel Field, in Terry, *Interviews and Recollections*, 188.

20 Gosse, in Maixner, *Critical Heritage*, 232.

21 James, *Partial Portraits*, 172.

22 James, in Maixner, *Critical Heritage*, 441.

23 Stevenson to Henry James, December 1893, 8:192–93.

24 Stevenson to W. E. Henley, July 17 or 18, 1883, 4:143–44.

25 Stevenson, "A Note on Realism," in *Essays of Travel and in the Art of Writing*, 280, 286.

26 Stevenson, "A Gossip on Romance," in Treglown, *The Lantern-Bearers*, 178.

27 Stevenson, "A Gossip on a Novel of Dumas's," in *Memories and Portraits*, 236.

28 Stevenson, "A Note on Realism," in *Essays of Travel and in the Art of Writing*, 285–86.

29 Stevenson, "The Lantern-Bearers," in Treglown, *The Lantern-Bearers*, 232.

30 Stevenson to Edmund Gosse, January 2, 1886, 5:172.

31 Stevenson, "Pulvis et Umbra," in *Across the Plains*, 298.

23 Stevenson, "Pastoral," in *Memories and Portraits*, 102.

......

33 Stevenson, "A Gossip on Romance," in Treglown, *The Lantern-Bearers*, 179.

34 Stevenson, "Pastoral," in *Memories and Portraits*, 102–3.

35 Stevenson, "A Humble Remonstrance," in Treglown, *The Lantern-Bearers*, 201.

36 Stevenson, "The Lantern-Bearers," in Treglown, *The Lantern-Bearers*, 230.

37 William James, quoted in Jack Barbalet, "WJ and Robert Louis Stevenson: The Importance of Emotion," *Streams of William James* 3.3 (Fall 2001), 6. http://journal.wjsociety.org/wp-content/uploads/2014/03/Streams_3.3.pdf.

38 Stevenson, "A Gossip on Romance," in Treglown, *The Lantern-Bearers*, 180.

39 James, *Partial Portraits*, 166.

40 Stevenson, "The Lantern-Bearers," in Treglown, *The Lantern-Bearers*, 235.

SIMPLICITY

1 Stevenson, *The Master of Ballantrae* (London: Penguin, 1996), 104.

2 Ibid., 8.

3 Isobel Field, in Terry, *Interviews and Recollections*, 187–88.

4 Stevenson, "The Genesis of *The Master of Ballantrae*," in Harman, *Essays and Poems*, 217.

5 Stevenson to Henry James, December 8, 1884, 5:42.

6 "Each, by his own method, seeks to save and perpetuate the same significance or charm: the one by suppressing, the other by forcing, detail." Stevenson to Bob Stevenson, September 30, 1883: 4:169.

7 Honoré de Balzac, *Père Goriot*, trans. Ellen Marriage (Mineola, NY: Dover Thrift, 2004), 4–5.

8 "Balzac and His Writings," *Westminster Review* 60 (1853), 211. https://babel.hathitrust.org/cgi/pt?id=uc1.c032045255;view=1up;seq=10.

9 Stevenson to Bob Stevenson, September 30, 1883, 4:169.

10 Isobel Field, in Terry, *Interviews and Recollections*, 188.

......

11 Stevenson, "A Note on Realism," in *Essays of Travel and in the Art of Writing*, 284.

12 Stevenson to Henry James, c. August 15, 1893, 8:152.

13 Stevenson, "A Note on Realism," in *Essays of Travel and in the Art of Writing*, 280.

14 Stevenson, "Victor Hugo's Romances," in *Familiar Studies of Men and Books* (New York: Scribner's, 1891), 39. http://www .archive.org/stream/familiarstudieso0stevuoft#page/n5 /mode/2up.

15 Stevenson to Charles Baxter, September 6, 1888, 6:207.

16 Stevenson, "A Note on Realism," in *Essays of Travel and in the Art of Writing*, 279.

17 Stevenson, "A Humble Remonstrance," in Treglown, *The Lantern-Bearers*, 200.

18 Stevenson to Frances Sitwell, October 5, 1873, 1:331.

19 Stevenson to Sidney Colvin, April 22, 1891, 7:102.

20 Stevenson to Edmund Gosse, April 1891, 7:105–6.

21 Stevenson, "On Some Technical Elements of Style," in *Essays of Travel and in the Art of Writing*, 258.

22 Adelaide Boodle, in Terry, *Interviews and Recollections*, 102.

23 Stevenson, "On Some Technical Elements of Style," in *Essays of Travel and in the Art of Writing*, 259.

24 Stevenson to John Williamson Palmer, February 13, 1885, 5:201.

25 Stevenson "The Morality of the Profession of Letters," in *Essays of Travel and in the Art of Writing*, 295.

26 Stevenson to John Williamson Palmer, February 13, 1886, 5:201.

27 Stevenson to Sidney Colvin, May 23, 1893, 8:72.

28 Stevenson to Bob Stevenson, October 9, 1883, 4:181.

29 Stevenson to William Archer, c. February 12, 1888, 6:113.

30 Stevenson, "A Gossip on Romance," in Treglown, *The Lantern-Bearers*, 175.

31 Ibid.

32 Stevenson, "Henry David Thoreau: His Character and Opinions," in *Familiar Studies of Men and Books*, 155–56.

33 Henry James, "The Art of Fiction," in *The Art of Criticism: Henry James on the Theory and Practice of Fiction*, ed. William Veeder and Susan M. Griffin (Chicago: University of Chicago Press, 1986), 173.

34 Stevenson, "A Humble Remonstrance," in Treglown, *The Lantern-Bearers*, 195, 200.

35 Stevenson to William Archer, c. February 12, 1888, 6:113.

36 Stevenson, "A Humble Remonstrance," in Treglown, *The Lantern-Bearers*, 200.

PLAY

1 Stevenson, "My First Book," in Harman, *Essays and Poems*, 211.

2 Stevenson to W. E. Henley, August 25, 1881, 3:225; September 1881, 3:230; August 25, 1881, 3:231, 229.

3 Stevenson to W. E. Henley, August 25, 1881, 3:225.

4 Stevenson, "My First Book," in Harman, *Essays and Poems*, 213–14.

5 Ibid., 210.

6 Ibid., 212, 214.

7 Ibid., 210.

8 Stevenson to Frances Sitwell, February 18, 1875, 2:119.

9 Stevenson to Edmund Gosse, June 10, 1893, 8:103.

10 Stevenson to Charles Baxter, September 9, 1894, 8:367.

11 Stevenson to Sidney Colvin, August 7, 1894, 8:343.

12 Stevenson, "Fontainebleau," in *Across the Plains*, 114.

13 Stevenson, "My First Book," in Harman, *Essays and Poems*, 209.

14 Stevenson to Edmund Gosse, January 2, 1886, 5:171.

15 Stevenson, "Letter to a Young Gentleman Who Proposes to Embrace the Career of Art," in Treglown, *The Lantern-Bearers*, 247.

16 Ibid., 249.

17 Ibid., 247.

18 Stevenson to Edmund Gosse, March 17, 1884, 4:261.

19 James, *Partial Portraits*, 145.

20 Edmund Gosse, *Critical Kit-Kats* (New York: Dodd, Mead, 1903), 145.

21 Stevenson to Thomas Stevenson, November 5, 1884, 5:20.

22 D. W. Winnicott, *Playing and Reality* (London: Routledge, 1971), 109.

23 Stevenson, "Letter to a Young Gentleman," in Treglown, *The Lantern-Bearers*, 245.

24 Stevenson, "A Gossip on Romance," in Treglown, *The Lantern-Bearers*, 182.

25 Stevenson to A. Trevor Haddon, June 1882, 3:333.

26 Stevenson, "Popular Authors," *Scribner's Magazine* 4.1 (July 1888): 124. http://ebooks.library.cornell.edu/cgi/t/text/page viewer-idx?c=scri;cc=scri;rgn=full%20text;idno=scri0004 -1;didno=scri0004-1;view=image;seq=0130;node=scri0004 -1%3A12.

27 Stevenson to Edmund Gosse, January 2, 1886, 5:171.

28 Stevenson, "Letter to a Young Gentleman," in Treglown, *The Lantern-Bearers*, 248.

29 Stevenson, "Books Which Have Influenced Me," in *Essays of Travel and in the Art of Writing*, 325.

30 Stevenson, "Fontainebleau," in *Across the Plains*, 141.

31 Stevenson, "Letter to a Young Gentleman," in Treglown, *The Lantern-Bearers*, 246.

READING

1 Stevenson to Angela Plomer, August 18, 1893, 8:154.

2 *Stevensoniana*, ed. John Alexander Hammerton (London: Grant Richards, 1903), 182–84.

3 Stevenson to George Saintsbury, March 4, 1886, 5:218.

4 Stevenson, "A College Magazine," in *Memories and Portraits*, 63.

5 Stevenson, "Random Memories: 'Rosa Quo Locorum,'" in *Essays of Travel and in the Art of Writing*, 216.

6 Stevenson to W. Leslie Curnow, January or February 1891, 7:82.

7   Stevenson, "A Gossip on Romance," in Treglown, *The Lantern-Bearers*, 172.

8   Stevenson to Sidney Colvin, May 20, 1892, 7:285.

9   Stevenson to J. M. Barrie, June 20, 1892, 7:315.

10 Stevenson to Ernest Rhys, August 11, 1894, 8:350.

11 Stevenson to Will H. Low, January 15, 1894, 8:235.

12 Stevenson to Ernest Rhys, August 11, 1894, 8:350.

13 Stevenson, "Books Which Have Influenced Me," in *Essays of Travel and in the Art of Writing*, 317.

14 Stevenson, "Preface, by Way of Criticism," in *Familiar Studies of Men and Books*, 8.

15 Stevenson, "Books Which Have Influenced Me," in *Essays of Travel and in the Art of Writing*, 325.

16 Ibid., 322.

17 Stevenson, "A Gossip on a Novel of Dumas's," in *Memories and Portraits*, 232.

18 Stevenson, "Books Which Have Influenced Me," in *Essays of Travel and in the Art of Writing*, 318.

19 Stevenson to John Addington Symonds, early March 1886, 5:221.

20 Stevenson, "Popular Authors,"128.

21 Ibid., 123.

22 Ibid., 128, 127.

23 Ibid., 127.

24 Stevenson, "Books Which Have Influenced Me," in *Essays of Travel and in the Art of Writing*, 318.

25 Ibid., 326.

26 Ibid.

27 Stevenson, "Preface, by Way of Criticism," in *Familiar Studies of Men and Books*, 26.

28 Stevenson, "Books Which Have Influenced Me," in *Essays of Travel and in the Art of Writing*, 324–25.

TRUTH

1   Stevenson, "The Morality of the Profession of Letters," in *Essays of Travel and in the Art of Writing*, 290–91.

......

2   Stevenson, "A Gossip on a Novel of Dumas's," in *Memories and Portraits*, 238.

3   Stevenson, "On Some Technical Elements of Style," in *Essays of Travel and in the Art of Writing*, 291.

4   Stevenson, "The Morality of the Profession of Letters," in *Essays of Travel and in the Art of Writing*, 291, 300, 291.

5   Stevenson to Thomas Stevenson, February 15, 2:240.

6   Stevenson to Bob Stevenson, October 1872, 1:254.

7   Stevenson to Arthur Patchett Martin, December 1877, 2:229.

8   Stevenson, "Samuel Pepys," in Harman, *Essays and Poems*, 126, 114.

9   Stevenson, "Walt Whitman," in Harman, *Essays and Poems*, 143.

10 Michel de Montaigne, "To the Reader," in *The Complete Essays of Montaigne*, trans. Donald Frame (Stanford: Stanford University Press, 1965), 2.

11 Stevenson, "A Christmas Sermon," in *Across the Plains*, 311.

12 Stevenson to W. E. Henley, December 4, 1884, 5:39–40.

13 Stevenson to Will H. Low, October 27, 1883, 4:196.

14 Stevenson, "The Morality of the Profession of Letters," in *Essays of Travel and in the Art of Writing*, 300.

15 Stevenson to Theodore Watts-Dunton, early September 1886, 5:314; to W. E. Henley, c. October 25, 1885, 5:140.

16 Stevenson, "The Morality of the Profession of Letters," in *Essays of Travel and in the Art of Writing*, 299.

17 Stevenson, "Truth of Intercourse," in Treglown, *The Lantern-Bearers*, 93.

18 Stevenson, "The Morality of the Profession of Letters," in *Essays of Travel and in the Art of Writing*, 298.

19 Stevenson, "A Gossip on a Novel of Dumas's," in *Memories and Portraits*, 238.

20 Ibid., 296.

21 Stevenson, "Lay Morals," in *Lay Morals and Other Papers* (New York: Charles Scribner's Sons, 1915), 3. https://archive.org/stream/laymoralsandothoostevgoog#page/n4/mode/2up.

22 Stevenson, "Books Which Have Influenced Me," in *Essays of Travel and in the Art of Writing*, 323.

23 Edward Purcell, in Maixner, *Critical Heritage*, 195.

24 Stevenson to Edward Purcell, February 27, 1886, 5:213.

25 Stevenson, "Some Aspects of Robert Burns," in Treglown, *The Lantern-Bearers*, 111, 117, 116, 120.

26 Ibid., 107.

27 Stevenson, "Preface, by Way of Criticism," in *Familiar Studies of Men and Books*, 15.

28 Stevenson, "Some Aspects of Robert Burns," in Treglown, *The Lantern-Bearers*, 124, 103, 121.

29 Stevenson, "A Christmas Sermon," in *Across the Plains*, 307–8.

30 Stevenson, "Markheim," in *The Complete Stories of Robert Louis Stevenson*, ed. Barry Menikoff (New York: Modern Library, 2002), 406.

31 Stevenson to W. E. Henley, early April 1879, 2:310.

32 Stevenson, "An Apology for Idlers," in Treglown, *The Lantern-Bearers*, 36.

33 Stevenson to Harriet Monroe, June 30, 1886, 5:272.

34 Stevenson, "The Morality of the Profession of Letters," in *Essays of Travel and in the Art of Writing*, 297.

TEACHING

1 Stevenson, "Some Aspects of Robert Burns," in Treglown, *The Lantern-Bearers*, 124–25.

2 Edward Eggleston, quoted in Hammerton, *Stevensoniana*, 301.

3 Hammerton, *Stevensoniana*, 143.

4 Stevenson, "On Talk and Talkers (I)," in Harman, *Essays and Poems*, 153. There are two chapters in Harman: "Talk and Talkers (I)" and "Talk and Talkers (II)."

5 Unsigned review, in Maixner, *Critical Heritage*, 78.

6 William Archer, in Maixner, *Critical Heritage*, 164, 288.

7 George Saintsbury, in Maixner, *Critical Heritage*, 95.

8 Archer, in Maixner, *Critical Heritage*, 288, 169.

9 Moore, in Maixner, *Critical Heritage*, 476–77; Purcell, *Critical*

Heritage, 195; Barrie, *Critical Heritage*, 414; Chapman,
Critical Heritage, 490–91.

10 Moore, in Maixner, *Critical Heritage*, 477.

11 Chesterton, *Robert Louis Stevenson*, 49.

12 Chesterton, in Maixner, *Critical Heritage*, 506.

13 Archer, in Maixner, *Critical Heritage*, 165.

14 Stevenson to William Archer, postmarked November 1, 1885,
5:149–50.

15 Stevenson to William Archer, October 30, 1885, 5:147–48.

16 Stevenson, "Crabbed Age and Youth," in Treglown, *The
Lantern-Bearers*, 68.

17 Eve Kosofsky Sedgwick, *Touching Feeling: Affect, Pedagogy,
Performativity* (Durham, NC: Duke University Press, 2003),
165.

18 Stevenson, "Walt Whitman," in Harman, *Essays and Poems*,
137.

19 Stevenson, "Lay Morals," in *Lay Morals and Other Papers*, 30.

20 Christopher Bollas, *Being a Character: Psychoanalysis and
Self Experience* (London: Routledge, 2003), 20.

21 Stevenson, "Lay Morals," in *Lay Morals and Other Papers*, 31.

22 Ibid., 35.

23 Stevenson, "Walt Whitman," in Harman, *Essays and Poems*,
137.

24 Stevenson, "Lay Morals," in *Lay Morals and Other Papers*,
35–36.

25 Archer, in Maixner, *Critical Heritage*, 165.

26 Montaigne, "Of Repentance," in *Complete Essays*, 612.

27 Stevenson, "The Morality of the Profession of Letters," in
Essays of Travel and in the Art of Writing, 300.

28 Stevenson, "Walt Whitman," in Harman, *Essays and Poems*,
137.

29 Stevenson, "Some Gentlemen in Fiction," 768.

30 Stevenson, "Books Which Have Influenced Me," in *Essays of
Travel and in the Art of Writing*, 319.

31 Stevenson, "El Dorado," in *Virginibus Puerisque and Other
Papers*, 190; *Travels with a Donkey*, 35, 5.

32 For a list of spurious quotes attributed to Stevenson, see
    http://www.robert-louis-stevenson.org/richard-dury-archive
    /nonquotes.htm.

33 James, *Partial Portraits*, 144.

34 Stevenson, "Lay Morals," in *Lay Morals and Other Papers*, 3.

35 Stevenson, "An Apology for Idlers," in Treglown, *The Lantern-
    Bearers*, 38. My italics.

STYLE

1   Moore, in Maixner, *Critical Heritage*, 329; Henley, *Critical
    Heritage*, 98; Grant Allen, *Critical Heritage*, 65.

2   Stevenson, "On Some Technical Elements of Style," in *Essays
    of Travel and in the Art of Writing*, 278.

3   Unsigned review, quoted in *Walter Pater: The Critical
    Heritage*, ed. R. M. Seiler (London: Routledge & Kegan Paul,
    1980), 199.

4   Stevenson to Richard Le Gallienne, December 28, 1893,
    8:212.

5   Stevenson, "On Some Technical Elements of Style," in *Essays
    of Travel and in the Art of Writing*, 255.

6   Stevenson, "A Note on Realism," in *Essays of Travel and in the
    Art of Writing*, 281.

7   Stevenson, "On Some Technical Elements of Style," in *Essays
    of Travel and in the Art of Writing*, 281.

8   Ibid., 282.

9   Stevenson to Edmund Gosse, November 9, 1881, 3:246–47.

10 Barry Menikoff, "Stevenson in the OED," in *Complete Stories*,
    811–18.

11 Stevenson to W. E. Henley, [July 4, 1882?] 3:338.

12 Andrew Lang, quoted in Terry, *Interviews and Recollections*,
    59.

13 Flora Masson, quoted in Terry, *Interviews and Recollections*,
    34.

14 Stevenson, in Smith, *Collected Poems*, 487, 469.

15 Stevenson to Edmund Gosse, July 24, 1879, 2:328.

16 Stevenson, in Smith, *Collected Poems*, 145.

17 Stevenson to Sidney Colvin, May 13, 1893, 7:281.

18 Stevenson to Sidney Colvin, January 17, 1891, 7:77.

19 Stevenson, "Across the Plains," in *Across the Plains*, 12.

20 Stevenson, "On Some Technical Elements of Style," in *Essays of Travel and in the Art of Writing*, 276.

21 Stevenson, "Truth of Intercourse," in Treglown, *The Lantern-Bearers*, 93.

22 Ibid., 94.

23 Ibid., 97.

24 Stevenson, "Random Memories: The Coast of Fife," in *Across the Plains*, 180–81.

25 Stevenson, "Beggars," in *Across the Plains*, 255–63.

26 Ibid.

27 Stevenson, "Lay Morals," in *Lay Morals and Other Papers*, 10.

28 James, *Partial Portraits*, 142.

29 Stevenson, "A Note on Realism," in *Essays of Travel and in the Art of Writing*, 282.

DREAMS

1 Stevenson, in Smith, *Collected Poems*, 371.

2 Stevenson, "Memoirs of Himself," in *The Works of Robert Louis Stevenson*, 26:214–15.

3 Stevenson, *Collected Poems*, 398.

4 Ibid., 380.

5 Ibid., 363.

6 Ibid., 402.

7 Ibid., 391.

8 Ibid., 383.

9 Ibid., 396.

10 Stevenson, "Memoirs of Himself," in *The Works of Robert Louis Stevenson*, 26:217–18.

11 Stevenson to Owen Wister, February 6, 1888, 6:109.

12 Charlotte Eaton, quoted in Terry, *Interviews and Recollections*, 137.

13 Stevenson to William Archer, March 29, 1885, 5:97.

14 Stevenson, in Smith, *Collected Poems*, 373.

15 Ibid., 387.

16 Stevenson to Sir Walter Simpson, [November 5, 1884?] 5:21.

17 Stevenson, in Smith, *Collected Poems*, 376.

18 Stevenson to W. E. Henley, [April 18, 1882?] 3:327.

19 Ibid., 402.

20 Stevenson to Alison Cunningham, February 16, 1883, 4:76.

21 Stevenson, "A Chapter on Dreams," in Treglown, *The Lantern-Bearers*, 217.

22 Ibid.

23 Ibid.

24 Quoted in Graham Balfour, *The Life of Robert Louis Stevenson* (New York: Scribner's, 1901), 1:38.

25 Stevenson, "Stormy Nights" and "Windy Nights," in Smith, *Collected Poems*, 86–88, 366.

26 Stevenson to Frances Sitwell, October 21, 1874, 2:66.

27 Quoted in Balfour, *Life*, 1:38.

28 Margaret Stevenson, "Diary," in R. L. Stevenson, *The Works of Robert Louis Stevenson*, 26:292.

29 Ibid., 26:279.

30 Stevenson, "A Chapter on Dreams," in Treglown, *The Lantern-Bearers*, 217.

31 Quoted in Hammerton, *Stevensoniana*, 85.

32 Stevenson, "A Chapter on Dreams," in Treglown, *The Lantern-Bearers*, 219–20.

33 Ibid., 224–25.

34 Quoted in Claire Harman, *Myself and the Other Fellow: A Life of Robert Louis Stevenson* (New York: Harper Perennial, 2005), 295–96.

35 Stevenson to F. W. H. Meyers, March 1, 1886, 5:216.

36 Stevenson, "A Chapter on Dreams," in Treglown, *The Lantern-Bearers*, 224.

37 Stevenson to F. W. H. Meyers, July 14, 1892, 7:331–34.

38 Stevenson, *Strange Case of Dr. Jekyll and Mr. Hyde* (Oxford: Oxford University Press, 2006), 55. My italics.

39 Vladimir Nabokov, "The Strange Case of Dr. Jekyll and Mr.

Hyde," in *Lectures on Literature* (New York: Harcourt Brace Jovanovich, 1980), 180.

40 Stevenson, *Jekyll and Hyde*, 26.

41 Ibid., 22.

42 Stevenson to Sidney Colvin, January 14, 1875, 2:107.

43 Balfour, *Life*, 1:167.

44 Stevenson to Sidney Colvin, January 14, 1875, 2:107.

BIBLIOGRAPHY

Balfour, Graham. *The Life of Robert Louis Stevenson.* 2 vols. New York: Charles Scribner's Sons, 1901.

"Balzac and His Writings," *Westminster Review* 60 (1853), 199–214. https://babel.hathitrust.org/cgi/pt?id=uc1.c032045255 ;view=1up;seq=10.

Balzac, Honoré de. *Père Goriot.* Translated by Ellen Marriage. Mineola, NY: Dover Thrift, 2004.

Barbalet, Jack. "WJ and Robert Louis Stevenson: The Importance of Emotion." *Streams of William James* 3.3 (Fall 2001): 6–9. http://journal.wjsociety.org/wp-content /uploads/2014/03/Streams_3.3.pdf.

Benjamin, Walter. "The Storyteller." In *Illuminations,* translated by Harry Zohn, 83–109. New York: Schocken Books, 1969.

Bollas, Christopher. *Being a Character: Psychoanalysis and Self Experience.* London: Routledge, 2003.

Booth, Bradford A., and Ernest Mayhew, eds. *The Letters of Robert Louis Stevenson.* 8 vols. New Haven: Yale University Press, 1995.

Chesterton, G. K. *Robert Louis Stevenson.* New York: Hodder and Stoughton, 1927.

———. *Varied Types.* New York: Dodd, Mead, 1901.

Gosse, Edmund. *Critical Kit-Kats.* New York: Dodd, Mead, 1903. https://archive.org/details/criticalkitkats01gossgoog.

Hammerton, J. A., ed. *Stevensoniana.* London: Grant Richards, 1903.

Harman, Claire. *Myself and the Other Fellow: A Life of Robert Louis Stevenson.* New York: Harper Perennial, 2005.

———, ed. *R. L. Stevenson: Essays and Poems.* London: Everyman, 1992.

James, Henry. "The Art of Fiction." In *The Art of Criticism: Henry James on the Theory and Practice of Fiction,* edited by William

Veeder and Susan M. Griffin, 165–96. Chicago: University of Chicago Press, 1986.

———. *Partial Portraits.* Westport, CT: Greenwood, 1970.

Maixner, Paul, ed. *Robert Louis Stevenson: The Critical Heritage.* London: Routledge & Kegan Paul, 1981.

Mantel, Hilary. "Art of Fiction No. 226." Interview by Mona Simpson. *Paris Review* 212 (Spring 2015): 36–71. https://www.theparisreview.org/interviews/6360/hilary-mantel-art-of-fiction-no-226-hilary-mantel.

Menikoff, Barry, ed. *The Complete Stories of Robert Louis Stevenson.* New York: Modern Library, 2002.

Montaigne, Michel de. *The Complete Essays of Montaigne.* Translated by Donald Frame. Stanford: Stanford University Press, 1965.

Nabokov, Vladimir. "The Strange Case of Dr. Jekyll and Mr. Hyde." In *Lectures on Literature*, 179–206. New York: Harcourt Brace Jovanovich, 1980.

Sedgwick, Eve Kosofsky. *Touching Feeling: Affect, Pedagogy, Performativity.* Durham, NC: Duke University Press, 2003.

Seiler, R. M. *Walter Pater: The Critical Heritage.* London: Routledge & Kegan Paul, 1980.

Smith, Janet Adam, ed. *Robert Louis Stevenson: Collected Poems.* New York: Viking, 1971.

Stevenson, Margaret. "Notes about Robert Louis Stevenson from his Mother's Diary." In R. L. Stevenson, *The Works of Robert Louis Stevenson*, 26:285–366.

Stevenson, Robert Louis. *Across the Plains.* London: Chatto & Windus, 1892. https://archive.org/stream/withoostevacrossplainsrich#page/n5/mode/2up.

———. "Across the Plains." In *Across the Plains*, 1–76.

———. "An Apology for Idlers." In Treglown, *The Lantern-Bearers*, 35–42.

———. "Books Which Have Influenced Me." In *Essays of Travel and in the Art of Writing*, 317–26.

———. "A Chapter on Dreams." In Treglown, *The Lantern-Bearers*, 216–225.

————. "A Christmas Sermon." In *Across the Plains*, 302–17.

————. "A College Magazine." In *Memories and Portraits*, 57–76.

————. "Crabbed Age and Youth." In Treglown, *The Lantern-Bearers*, 59–68.

————. "Diogenes." In *The Works of Robert Louis Stevenson*, 26:7–18.

————. *Edinburgh: Picturesque Notes*. London: Pallas, 2001.

————. "The Education of an Engineer." In Treglown, *The Lantern-Bearers*, 251–58.

————. "El Dorado." In *Virginibus Puerisque and Other Papers*, 172–78.

————. *Essays of Travel and in the Art of Writing*. New York: Charles Scribner's Sons, 1905. https://archive.org/stream /essaysoftravelinoostev#page/n5/mode/2up.

————. *Familiar Studies of Men and Books*. New York: Charles Scribner's Sons, 1891. http://www.archive.org/stream /familiarstudiesoostevuoft#page/n5/mode/2up.

————. "Fontainebleau." In *Across the Plains*, 108–42.

————. "The Foreigner at Home." In Harman, *R. L. Stevenson: Essays and Poems*, 13–21.

————. "The Genesis of *The Master of Ballantrae*." In Harman, *R. L. Stevenson: Essays and Poems*, 217–19.

————. "A Gossip on a Novel of Dumas's." In *Memories and Portraits*, 228–46.

————. "A Gossip on Romance." In Treglown, *The Lantern-Bearers*, 172–82.

————. "Henry David Thoreau: His Character and Opinions." In *Familiar Studies of Men and Books*, 137–73.

————. "A Humble Remonstrance." In Treglown, *The Lantern-Bearers*, 192–201.

————. *Kidnapped*. Oxford: Oxford University Press, 2014.

————. *"Kidnapped" and "Catriona."* Oxford: Oxford University Press, 1986.

————. *Lay Morals and Other Papers*. New York: Charles Scribner's Sons, 1915. https://archive.org/stream/laymorals andothoostevgoog#page/n4/mode/2up.

———. "Letter to a Young Gentleman Who Proposes to Embrace the Career of Art." In Treglown, *The Lantern-Bearers*, 244–50.

———. "Markheim." In Menikoff, *The Complete Stories of Robert Louis Stevenson*, 393–409.

———. *The Master of Ballantrae*. London: Penguin, 1996.

———. "Memoirs of Himself." In *The Works of Robert Louis Stevenson*, 26:226.

———. *Memories and Portraits*. New York: Charles Scribner's Sons, 1895. https://archive.org/details/memoriesand portroostev.

———. "The Morality of the Profession of Letters." In *Essays of Travel and in the Art of Writing*, 286–301.

———. "My First Book: *Treasure Island*." In Harman, *R. L. Stevenson: Essays and Poems*, 209–16.

———. "A Note on Realism." In *Essays of Travel and in the Art of Writing*, 278–86.

———. "On Some Technical Elements of Style in Literature." In *Essays of Travel and in the Art of Writing*, 253–77.

———. "Pastoral." In *Memories and Portraits*, 90–105.

———. "'A Penny Plain and Twopence Coloured.'" In Harman, *R. L. Stevenson: Essays and Poems*, 63–68.

———. "A Plea for Gas Lamps." In *Virginibus Puerisque and Other Papers*, 288–96.

———. "Popular Authors." *Scribner's Magazine* 4:1 (July 1888). http://ebooks.library.cornell.edu/cgi/t/text/pageviewer-idx?c=scri;cc=scri;rgn=full%20text;idno=scri0004-1;didno=scri0004-1;view=image;seq=0130;node=scri0004-1%3A12.

———. "Preface, by Way of Criticism." In *Familiar Studies of Men and Books*, 7–26.

———. "Pulvis et Umbra." In *Across the Plains*, 289–301.

———. "Random Memories: The Coast of Fife." In *Across the Plains*, 168–88.

———. *The Silverado Squatters*. London: Chatto & Windus, 1910. https://archive.org/stream/silveradosquasteoostev#page/n9/mode/2up.

———. "Some Aspects of Robert Burns." In Treglown, *The Lantern-Bearers*, 100–25.

———. "Some Gentlemen in Fiction." *Scribner's Magazine*, June 1888. http://ebooks.library.cornell.edu/cgi/t/text/pageviewer-idx?c=scri;cc=scri;rgn=full%20text;idno=scri0003-6;didno=scri0003-6;view=image;seq=0772;node=scri0003-6%3A14.

———. *Strange Case of Dr. Jekyll and Mr. Hyde*. Oxford: Oxford University Press, 2006.

———. *Travels with a Donkey in the Cévennes*. New York: Penguin, 2004.

———. "Truth of Intercourse." In Treglown, *The Lantern-Bearers*, 93–99.

———. "Victor Hugo's Romances." In *Familiar Studies of Men and Books*, 27–58.

———. *Virginibus Puerisque and Other Papers*. London: C. Kegan Paul, 1881. http://www.archive.org/stream/buspuerisstevvirginirich#page/n5/mode/2up.

——— . "Walt Whitman." In Harman, *R. L. Stevenson: Essays and Poems*, 133–52.

———. *The Works of Robert Louis Stevenson*, Vailima Edition. 26 vols. New York: Charles Scribner's Sons, 1923.

Terry, M. C., ed. *Robert Louis Stevenson: Interviews and Recollections*. Iowa City: University of Iowa Press, 1996.

Treglown, Jeremy, ed. *The Lantern-Bearers and Other Essays*. New York: Farrar, Straus & Giroux, 1988.

Winnicott, D. W. *Playing and Reality*. London: Routledge, 1971.

INDEX